M000191175

THE LIFE OF CHRISTINA OF HANE

The Life of Christina of Hane

Translation, Introduction,
and Annotation by

Racha Kirakosian

Yale

UNIVERSITY PRESS

New Haven and London

Published with assistance from the Louis Stern Memorial Fund.

Yale University Press books may be purchased in quantity
for educational, business, or promotional use. For information,
please email sales.press@yale.edu (U.S. office) or
sales@yaleup.co.uk (U.K. office).

Designed and set in Adobe Caslon type by Karen Stickler.
Printed in the United States of America.

Library of Congress Control Number: 2020932746
ISBN 978-0-300-25099-2 (hardcover : alk. paper)

A catalogue record for this book is available from the British Library.

This paper meets the requirements of ANSI/NISO Z39.48-1992
(Permanence of Paper).

10 9 8 7 6 5 4 3 2 1

For David William Hughes

Contents

Preface   ix

Introduction   xiii

Map and illustrations   lvii

The Life of Christina of Hane   1

Notes   99

References   125

Further Reading   137

Index   141

Preface

When one thinks of medieval mystics, names such as Julian of Norwich, Margery Kempe, Henry Suso, and Gertrude the Great may come to mind. The thirteenth-century mystic Christina of Hane, a Premonstratensian canoness, deserves to be added to this list of influential thinkers. With this translation her recently unearthed case can now be "discovered" by Anglophone readers. Christina's visions hark back to a monastic tradition of ascetic practices; at the same time, her *Life* is unusual in many ways: her severe self-punitive vaginal mutilation, her stigmata, her equivalence to the Virgin Mary, her quasi-heretical statements about the union with Christ, and her elaborate relationship to music are but a few particularities worth highlighting. *The Life of Christina of Hane* challenges existing assumptions about female gendered authorship, vernacular theology, medieval sexuality, and the relationship between vision and liturgy in unique ways. Indebted to a manuscript culture in which texts developed dynamically, the *Life* connects aspects of performativity on the text's surface with a mystical program of becoming the bride of Christ. Readers will hopefully find it fascinating and insightful for different kinds of studies pertaining to history, philosophy, historical anthropology, body politics, gender studies, theology, and the study of religion.

You never get to know a text as well as when you translate it; that is, when you are responsible for its rendering into another language while retaining the semantic, grammatical, poetic, rhetorical, and cultural nuances specific to the original. Yet any translation is a kind of redaction and a new text in its own right. No wonder, then, that—with such complex processes at the bottom of it—a translation can rarely be the outcome of one single mind. This book would have been impossible without the collective effort of many people.

My dear colleagues and friends Almut Suerbaum, Nigel Palmer, Jeffrey Hamburger, Laura Nasrallah, CJ Jones, Ann Marie Rasmussen, Barbara Newman, Constance Furey, Annette Volfing, Nicholas Watson, and Amy Hollywood have accompanied this project at different stages, lending it the matchless polish of their attention and expertise. With heartfelt gratitude I thank them all for having kindly and patiently helped and encouraged me over the past years to complete the translation of and introduction to *The Life of Christina of Hane*. I would also like to thank my diligent research assistants Hans Pech, Jonas Hermann, and Manuel Gebhardt for their time and energy.

Many thanks go to the Faculty of Arts and Sciences at Harvard University, which has employed me during the course of translating the *Life*, and to the Swedish Collegium for Advanced Study, where I was a fellow during the publication process. I also owe thanks to the Bibliothèque nationale et universitaire de Strasbourg, Count von Oppersdorff Solms-Braunfels, the Municipal Archive of Mechelen, and Harvard's digital cartographer

Scott Walker for their generosity. Special thanks are reserved for the brilliant editor Heather Gold: it was a real delight to work with her. No less gratitude goes to Annie Imbornoni, whose help in the proof stage was invaluable.

I am also grateful to Bobbi Koz Paley, whose peaceful house in the countryside offered important writing retreats, and to Francesca Southerden, with whom I had the pleasure to live during the first drafts of this translation. Last but not least I thank my husband, David William Hughes, to whom this book is dedicated: without his steadfast support and his unfaltering font of knowledge and wisdom I would have never finished it.

Racha Kirakosian
Uppsala, September 2019

Introduction

Christina of Hane (1269–1292?) is the only known medieval female mystic of the Premonstratensian Order. *The Life of Christina of Hane,* which tells us about her, begins like a traditional saint's life, but as one scholar of mysticism has remarked, it "offers surprises—unique peculiarities—to the reader who expects nothing other than analogies to known types."[1] Both textually and in terms of content we find unparalleled complexity as an ascetic program of mortification of the flesh, the union of the soul and God, and the cosmos of divine creation are unfolded in a combination of hagiographic narrative, mystical dialogue, and theological reflection.[2] Research into the "peculiarities" of the *Life* has just begun, and many aspects are yet to be fully studied.[3]

It seems at first exceptional that a Premonstratensian canoness should be at the center of a mystical hagiography; beguines and Dominican and Franciscan nuns are better known for participating in the mystical discourses of the thirteenth to fifteenth centuries. Yet Christina of Hane was not the first of her order to have been active in mystical spirituality. Hermann Joseph of Steinfeld (c. 1155–1250?)—thought to have authored the oldest known hymn to the Heart of Jesus—was a canon prominent for his Marian devotion inspired by Bernard of Clairvaux's language of bridal mysticism.[4] Hermann Joseph was connected to the female mystics of his time through his role as spiritual overseer for women's convents.[5] He was also acquainted with the *Revelations* of Elisabeth of Schönau,[6] a text that may have been known to the hagiographer of Christina of Hane as well. It is even more likely that Hermann Joseph's writings themselves were sources for the *Life* because we can see parallels between his mysticism and that of Christina of Hane—in particular, the focus on the individual soul, the trope of playing with the Christ Child, and the climactic mystical union described in nuptial terms (the trope of *connubium*). Although we can regard Hermann Joseph as a "mystical precursor" in the Premonstratensian Order, one cannot speak of a particular medieval mystical tradition among the Norbertines.[7] It is nevertheless striking that while the Premonstratensian Order is primarily renowned for its male members, who received a rigorous training, especially in matters concerning the liturgy and music, with Christina of Hane we encounter a canoness who appears to be engaged in mystical thought as well as liturgical music. That the canonesses to some extent profited from such a training can be seen in the exceptional mysticism that Christina of Hane offers.

A unique source for medieval culture and spirituality, her *Life,* an intricate text that surpasses genre boundaries, gives us new insights into the spiritual practices and mystical beliefs of the high and late Middle Ages. The oldest source telling us about Christina of Hane is a late fifteenth- or early sixteenth-century copy of her medieval *Life* as found in a manuscript kept today at the National and University Library of Strasbourg (Strasbourg, Bibliothèque nationale et universitaire, MS 324). The text, albeit transmitted relatively late, has its roots in the thirteenth and fourteenth centuries: language and theological content attest to early stages of composition followed by later rewritings. The manuscript's rediscovery by Franz Paul Mittermaier in 1958 led to a series of new questions regarding the historical contexts of both the text and the person it concerns. The following exposition serves to highlight the characteristics of the *Life* with special consideration of its historical embeddedness.

THE HAGIOGRAPHY OF CHRISTINA OF HANE

All that we know about Christina of Hane comes from her *Life*, according to which she entered the Premonstratensian convent in Hane in 1275 at the age of six. The order was founded by Norbert of Xanten in 1120 and follows the Rule of St. Augustine. The men of the order receive clerical training and are called canons; the women are accordingly referred to as canonesses.[8] Hane, located in the Palatinate, a densely forested, mountainous region in the Upper Rhine area to the northeast of Alsace (see map), was a women's convent under the supervision of the canons of Rothenkirchen; it is also the place where an extraordinary woman named Christina is said to have had a special relationship with God. Christina was very likely the daughter of a highborn official, probably connected to the counts of Nassau,[9] who in turn were related to the counts of Bolanden (Count Werner I of Bolanden had founded the convent of Hane in 1129).[10] She may have been a younger sister of the German king Adolf of Nassau (c. 1250–1298/r. 1292–1298), but the scattered information we have about her biological family does not allow firm conclusions as to her background.[11] She was probably learned in Latin as her visions containing Latin language as well as her active participation in the liturgy suggest. The fact that at one instance the *Life* indicates that she did not know Latin (Ch. 10) may be connected to a common trope of humility, as found for example in Mechthild of Magdeburg's *Flowing Light of the Godhead.*[12]

The first part of Christina's life, written in a hagiographic style with a narrator oscillating between narrative and discursive voices, is influenced by ascetic practices that are rooted in a monastic tradition. While still a child Christina stands out among her convent peers, not joining in with their games but instead contemplating Christ's childhood and the ephemerality of human existence. The *Life* specifies that at the age of ten Christina joins the convent school to be trained for participation in the daily office. Three years later she and other members have to leave the community because of financial struggles it is facing.[13] After six months living back with her family, Christina returns to Hane and finds herself afflicted by temptations, especially ones of a sexual nature. Although Christina's temptations are portrayed as proof of her sanctity, the *Life* details a severe seven-year-long self-punitive program to combat the seven cardinal sins. Her zeal and the amazement it causes among those who witness it remind us of Thomas of Cantimpré's *Life of Christina the Astonishing*, known in the Middle Ages as Christina Mirabilis (c. 1150–1224).[14] In general, Christina of Hane's ascetic measures are reminiscent of those of the Desert Fathers and bear hagiographic immanence, yet her suffering as juxtaposed to the soul's spiritual enjoyment of the union with the divine echoes contemporary mystics, among whom we may count, in addition to Christina Mirabilis, the Dominican Elsbeth von Oye (c. 1280–1350), who in her own life record detailed multifarious self-harming exercises.[15] What stands out in Christina of Hane's self-harm as extremely unusual, however, is the maltreatment of her genitals, in particular of her vagina. Christina pushes a burning woodblock into her vagina, and introduces first a vinegar and chalk mixture into it, then a urine and chalk mixture, in order to put an end to lust.[16] Her anti-lecherous operations and the way the resulting symptoms are described suggest that there was knowledge about the clitoris as an erogenous zone—a comprehension of female genitalia to be found nowhere else in medieval Europe.[17] Christina's programmatic battle against vice is partnered with a subsequent cultivation of Christian virtues. According to the *Life*, once Christina's soul has reached perfection through this program, she leads the life of a visionary.

Only a few dates are mentioned in the *Life* (Christina's entry into the convent in 1275, and visions on Easter 1288, Christmas 1288, and Epiphany 1289), but we can infer that early in 1288 Christina becomes very ill and is henceforth bound to the sickbed. She suffers ailments early on, often self-inflicted: on one occasion, she stays up all night barefoot on the church's cold stone floor, succumbing to a fever as a consequence. Other prayer practices harm her body: in praying to the Virgin Mary, she injures her knees when she falls to the ground to follow the Angelus bell in her worship. Christina's creativity knows no bounds in devising means of self-chastisement: she buries her legs in snow, then beats them once they are stiff of cold; she uses a besom to flagellate herself, and puts nettles into her bed causing blisters all over her body. At several instances she comes close to death, and toward the end of her life she bears five wounds on her body mirroring the martyrdom of Christ (where the wounds are located is not specified in the *Life*). When exactly Christina dies is uncertain, as the *Life* is not explicit about her actual passing. Scholars have suggested 1292 as the end of her life on the basis of Christina's last vision and the sequence in which feast days are mentioned.[18]

Among her sisters in spirit, Christina is mostly respected and beloved, especially near her death—though the convent's prioress (called "magistra" in Premonstratensian convents of the time) sometimes physically punishes Christina for her prayer practices, which are deemed excessive. We also hear that another canoness speaks harsh words to Christina, which she chooses not to return, instead biting her own tongue, thus forcing blood to pour out of her nose and mouth. Generally, however, her sisters take good care of her, and are extremely concerned for her health and well-being. Together with the "Brother," who appears to be the hagiographer, they are awe-struck by the severity of Christina's disease and the words she utters or sings during periods of unconsciousness.

Christina's mortified body becomes the stage of her sanctity: to those near her the miracle-like dying and reawakening is astounding, recalling as it does the Passion of Christ; to the reader, the juxtaposition of Christina's physical suffering and her inner rejoicing about the deliverance of souls in purgatory is enthralling. Numerous questions are provoked by these interplays between the flesh and the body, illness and salvation, choice and destiny. For example, how does the body transform from a cause of sin to a machine of redemption? How do spiritual exercises and virtuous conduct weigh into a predestined marriage of the soul with Christ? These and other inquiries invite the reader to explore Christina's *Life* in relation to the history of the body, spiritual history, and medieval culture at large.

Christina's abbot functions as her confessor, but whether he can be identified with the canon who supposedly wrote the *Life* is unclear. At one instance the narrator—who provides heavy commentary in the first, most hagiographic, section of the *Life*—states that he is a "Brother" who has witnessed Christina's ecstatic raptures and severe ailments. From the written style of the *Life*, scholars have inferred that its author must have been a cleric with a theological and scholastic education, who would have been Christina's confessor. This position of "confessor" at Hane would have been executed by one of the canons of the supervising convent in Rothenkirchen. Despite various concrete candidates, there is no consensus as to exactly who Christina's confessor and possible hagiographer was.[19] The initial author of the *Life* thus remains anonymous. Given the many shifts in the *Life* in style and tone, and the work's relatively late transmission (more than one hundred years after Christina's lifetime), we must assume more collective scenarios for its production and development over the centuries.[20]

VISIONS, MYSTICAL THEOLOGY, AND DYNAMIC TEXTUALITY

The *Life* draws heavily from liturgical sources, as seen in the numerous chants and feast days that are quoted. Scriptures, Church Fathers, and saints' lives are referred to directly and indirectly. Neoplatonic concepts are well explored, but their source is hard to determine given that bridal mysticism itself is grafted to early Christian theology in the tradition of Neoplatonic thinkers.[21] We may also speculate, though with a greater degree of certainty, about later medieval sources. Philosophical inserts from fourteenth-century debates made their way into the *Life*, suggesting that we are dealing with a multilayered process of copying and compiling. One extended vision of the divine heart (Ch. 21) hints at a possible reception of the Helfta mystics, who refined the motif around 1300. It may, however, be even older and form part of a reaction to the burgeoning cult of Corpus Christi, which also features in the *Life* (Ch. 22).[22] Occasional references to chivalry and chivalrous behavior (Chs. 15 and 18), as well as a battle scene with an allegorized Love (Ch. 21), are reminiscent of courtly love poetry. They could equally stem from a reception of the poetry of Mechthild of Magdeburg or Hadewijch. The geographical proximity of the Low Countries to the Palatinate, where the *Life* was compiled, may have favored a reception of Hadewijch's writings. This scenario is also plausible considering the similarity to other aspects of Hadewijch's writings, such as Eucharistic visions connected to consumption and bodily sensation (Ch. 22).

The *Life* begins in a hagiographic tone, transitions to a middle section largely consisting of direct speech from Christ, and ends with a treatise-like reflection on the Annunciation and its implications as told from the mystic's perspective. These various layers led Kurt Ruh, a scholar of medieval German mysticism, to conclude that the *Life* was composed or edited from different types of sources, and he assumed that the last part must have originated from a male author. According to Ruh, it is most unlikely that the visionary and mystic Christina would have known of theological matters, no matter how relevant they were to her own lifetime. It seemed unimaginable to him that a female voice would utter abstract concepts authoritatively, even more so in what was supposed to be her own saint's life, since the genre prescribes a narrative frame set by the hagiographer (and not by the saint).[23] Ruh's conclusion underlines the tension in the triadic relation between text type, gendered voice, and the themes inherent in the *Life*. Mystical theology hinges on all three of these aspects, and it is thus not surprising that Christina of Hane's case has been considered a particularly complex one. The following exploration seeks to unpack some of the issues posed by this text.

The *Life* shares features with other important hagiographic and mystical texts from medieval Europe. Like the texts related to the Helfta mystics Mechthild of Hackeborn (*Liber specialis gratiae*) and Gertrude of Helfta (*Legatus divinae pietatis*), the *Life*'s structure largely follows the liturgical calendar (in which specific feast days trigger particular visions). The vision of a celestial mass held concomitantly to the convent mass (Ch. 33) evokes a similarly overlayered mass described by Gertrude of Helfta (*Legatus* IV, 59).[24] As in the texts connected with Gertrude and Mechthild, and those connected with other mystics such as the Dominican nun Adelheid Langmann, Mechthild of Magdeburg, Angela of Foligno, and Catherine of Siena, the center of interest in the *Life* is an intimate relationship between the soul and her bridegroom Christ. Christina's desire to achieve union with Christ is linked to the Eucharist. Although the mystical union is often fulfilled—and repeatedly confirmed by Christ's voice as a union of the wills—the trope of the separation of the lovers is also present, employed especially in terms of affective language. By alluding to the allegorical understanding of the soul as the bride of the Song of Songs, the *Life* draws on a long tradition of spiritual and affective readings of this biblical text.[25] What is compelling about Christina's relationship to Christ is that their identities intertwine to the point of perfect union, which is repeatedly affirmed by Christ's voice. Insistence on the identity of wills (for example, Ch. 92), grammatically expressed in nestled formulations (for example, Chs. 67 and 71),[26] is potentially heretical, as it places Christina on a parallel with Christ and God.[27]

Christina has different types of visions, some of which are significant to both her immediate and her wider community. Christina's prophetic visions are all condensed in a series of revelations that provide her with insights into her own present time:[28]

for example, she sees where fellow canonesses hide figs (Ch. 23), how a man kills his wife (the same man subsequently brings the corpse to the convent for burial, which is refused him on the basis of Christina's prophecy, Ch. 25), and that various members of her biological family die (Chs. 23 and 26). Among her visions is also one that concerns the papal court: Christina sees falsehood and treachery at the curia (Ch. 23). With such a range of prophetic visions, reaching even into the political realm, Christina stands out as a particularly multifaceted visionary.

Her visions are also of a figurative nature, with vivid images that appear like vignettes. In one vision Christina sees a tree with Christ as a bird singing to other, smaller birds, *Ego sum panis vivus,* to which they reply, *Tu es panis vivus, in quo omnes vivimus in eternum* (Ch. 22). The imagery may be related to medieval depictions of Christ surrounded by birds, based on the allegory of the palm tree,[29] seen for example in the *Rothschild Canticles* (New Haven, Beinecke, MS 404, fol. 5r).[30] This codex from around 1300 is an example of the nexus created by mysticism, imagery, and vision, with meditation standing at the center of its visually defined devotional program.[31] The main difference between Christina's visionary account of the tree and the aforementioned manuscript illumination is that in the *Rothschild Canticles* Christ is depicted as crucified, whereas in Christina's vision he is an eagle-like bird. The motif of the eagle may well derive from the vision of two eagles in Ezekiel 17, which was read as a messianic topology in the Middle Ages. Other visions that Christina has featuring a tree (Chs. 30 and 31) or an eagle (Ch. 79) show that rather than assuming one particular source for this kind of imagery, we are more likely dealing with a media-mixing reception of different sources. For example, Christina's engagement with painted and drawn depictions of the crucifix is explicitly mentioned (Ch. 7). In sum, the visions may be understood as an artistic expression of meditative practices, in which images serve contemplative purposes.

Infused with hymns and antiphons, Christina's visions highlight the musically creative component of Christina's contemplation. Visions in *The Life of Christina of Hane* are often triggered by liturgical celebrations or prayer practices. Here, inner and outer sensory experiences intermingle within experiences of synesthesia, as music repeatedly appears in depictions of the union. The *Life* contains lyrical prose and rhymes, explicitly referred to as songs; angels and humans sing to worship God; Christ and Mary teach tunes whose words are specified; multivocal choirs sing in unison. In line with medieval music theory, music is portrayed as a celestial language, into which the terrestrial choirs can synchronically blend.[32] In manifold visions, in which Christina of Hane sees and/or hears Christ, aural perception of music becomes the catalyst for the manifestation of the divine as well as the result or actual outcome of such an experience. Although the *Life* does not transmit notated musical melodies (which is not surprising for a bridal mystical text), music still plays a pivotal role on different levels (discursive and poetic), showing that the mystic and her hagiographer had good knowledge of medieval music theory, which was tied to cosmological and theological questions.[33] The musical world described in visions is juxtaposed with Christina's mystical experiences, which were said to include and produce music: musical sound becomes a performative way to present and induce the mystical union. Thus, music in Christina's *Life* unites the terrestrial with the celestial realm in a performative way.[34]

What is special about Christina's visionary phenomenology (that is, how her senses relate to visions) is that while she experiences the liturgy on both levels—as earthly celebration and heavenly vision—at other times her senses are dead to her own voice or any physical stimulation. This differentiation in the visionary phenomenology shows a deep understanding of the liturgy, which meant to imitate celestial worship and thereby open to its participants a gateway to an eschatological realm.[35] Since Christina's visions during liturgical events include physical perception of her surroundings (for example, Ch. 33), the theoretical blending of terrestrial and celestial celebrations (the liturgical space as a stage for enacting the otherworld) is acted out in her visions during liturgical celebrations. During extraliturgical visions, however, everything Christina sees before her "inner eyes" she communicates to "those who [are] present," but without her own knowledge, meaning that she is unaware of her own "outward" utterances. At one such instance her eyes are wide open, further highlighting the discrepancy between inner vision and outer, sensory, experience (Ch. 57). Christina is described as being unaware of sensory perception when having this kind of vision. This state is as an ecstatic one: according to Augustine, during *ecstasis* bodily functions do not operate.[36] Furthermore, the *Life* specifies that she is enraptured during her visions, which is a common way to describe ecstasy. Other than prophetic visions, Christina has visions of the otherworld, in which she explores especially heaven (Ch. 37).[37] The vast majority of divine communications, however, concern her soul's relationship with Christ and the affirmation of her prayers as successful in liberating souls from purgatory.

The deliverance of souls from purgatory is another aspect Christina has in common with Christina Mirabilis, the importance of purgatory being paramount in the *Life:* Christina of Hane is a prolific liberator of souls who await the full redemption of their sins in this temporally defined space between death and eternal afterlife. Purgatory, from the late twelfth century onward, was thought to be a topographical and mental space of punishment and purification that offered the possibility of a prolonged process of penitence, extending the path to salvation beyond the actual death of the human body. Atonement in purgatory, though removed from the realm of the world, remained a corporeal form of purification. In the *Life,* the pain Christina suffers on these souls' behalf functions as a sort of ransom; in a way, she lends them her earthly body, which she has purged of sins.[38] By liberating thousands of souls from purgatory (Ch. 51, 56–58, 63, 70, 78, 83, 91, and 95), Christina is depicted as performing a service for the departed barely matched in the history of Western spirituality.[39]

While Christina can undoubtedly be described as a visionary and a mystic, the question of whether her *Life* offers an original mystical theology or a scholastic reception of mystical ideas is contentious, as it addresses many theoretical issues that are entangled with the status of vernacular theology and that of female mysticism. So-called female mystical literature is often generally subsumed under "vernacular theology"[40]—a categorization that inadvertently led to the language of a mystical text counting as the primary genre characteristic. This derivation is precarious because of the implicit distinction between Latin discourses of the male-dominated scholastic world and vernacular texts about supposedly practical experiences as reactions to the Scriptures and the daily office. That such binary views do not hold up against the complexity of medieval culture becomes particularly evident in the case of Christina of Hane.

As the *Life* progresses (from Ch. 97), auditions—divine communications that are primarily auditory rather than visionary—are directly presented through Christina's voice; the mediating narrator now ceases to introduce Christ as the speaker and disappears entirely behind Christina's first-person account. It is in this last part of the *Life* that the most pertinent philosophical questions, for example regarding the nature of the Trinity, are raised and discussed in new and original ways. One of these concerns the medieval theological debate on the primacy of knowledge, love, or enjoyment of God (Ch. 98). Traditionally, Franciscans held the position in favor of the will (love), while Dominicans stressed the intellect (knowledge). In scholastic Latin texts—such as the mid-thirteenth-century *Compendium theologicae veritatis* of the Dominican Hugh Ripelin of Strasbourg—the progression from knowledge to loving to possessing is raised in the context of the ascent to God.[41] The same debate was discussed by later speculative mystics such as Meister Eckhart, Ruusbroec, and Gisilher von Slatheim.[42] The *Life* opts for the equal importance of knowledge, love, and enjoyment, thus taking an individual position in relation to a scholastic discourse.[43]

Perhaps due to the relatively late transmission of the *Life*, we find more echoes of the mysticism of the Rhineland as it developed in the fourteenth century. In addition to the Neoplatonic concept of emanation, which is dominantly present in the *Life* with frequent expressions related to flowing (infusion and effusion), there are traces of an Eckhartian detachment, when in the *Life* the soul gets rid of herself and dies in God to become nameless (Ch. 100) and when Christ's voice commands Christina to let go of God for the sake of God (Ch. 59).[44] Such Eckhartian reverberations may lead us to believe, as Barbara Newman suggests, "that the ending of her [Christina's] Vita was added by a cleric familiar with Eckhart, who decided to use the saint as a mouthpiece for his ideas about mystical union."[45] Throughout the *Life*, theological statements reminiscent of fourteenth-century discourse make a case for a long-term rewriting process. For example, what has been thought to be a foreshadowing of Henry Suso's devotion to the Holy Wisdom in the *Life* (Ch. 29)[46] more likely belongs to a rather complex reception history of Dominican spiritual thought. More specifically, we can trace some of the statements made in the *Life* about the unmediated union of the will (in particular Ch. 78) to a text of *dicta* and *sententiae* related to Meister Eckhart, the so-called *Liber Positionum.*[47] Also, the use of the Middle High German word *mitewësen* in a treatise-like monologue on the unification of soul and God (Ch. 97) may well stem from a sermon by Eckhart for the Third Sunday of Advent.[48] In that sermon, Eckhart addresses the issues of angels as God's image and of God's essence—topics that are also prevalent in the *Life* (for example, Ch. 100). These—and more intertextual observations, further outlined in the notes to the translation below—corroborate the hypothesis that the *Life* belongs to a group of texts that were produced in a creative reaction to the ideas of Meister Eckhart and his followers. Although it is difficult to ascertain where exactly much of the speculative mysticism in the *Life* stems from, continuous influences on the scribes who copied the text material have undoubtedly found their way into the *Life* as it has come down to us.

No matter how much the *Life* might reverberate with other texts, including some that were produced after Christina of Hane's lifetime,[49] one particular theological aspect remains unique to the *Life:* the status of the soul in relation to the Virgin Mary, who herself is treated as the highest saint (Ch. 32). Christina somewhat equals Mary as the bride of Christ; the allegorical interpretation of the Song of Songs heightens this competition, and Christina's soul is finally crowned (Chs. 63 and 81) and enthroned (Chs. 35, 59, 74, and 81) as heavenly queen reigning over the nine angelic choirs (Ch. 63).[50] This cosmological position that Christina's soul inhabits is unmistakably reserved for Mary in the Christian tradition. On Marian feast days, Christ reveals the seven wisdoms (Ch. 29) and seven joys (Ch. 67) of Mary to Christina's soul, stylizing her as the *sedes sapientiae,* the Seat of Wisdom.[51] That Christina should be equivalent to the heavenly queen is already hinted at toward the beginning of the *Life,* where an extended allegory compares her to the biblical figure of Esther by means of a typological relationship that sets Christina as a savior of many in her capacity as heavenly queen (Ch. 1). Christina's ailments and stigmata, her life as "a living sacrifice," to borrow Paul's words from the Letter to the Romans, moreover proves her Marian function as a co-redemptrix who liberates countless souls from purgatory.

One peculiarity shows an unorthodox treatment of the Virgin Mary when it comes to mystical texts: during Christina's devotional practices in front of a sculpture of Mary, the sculpture becomes animated, extends its hand, and slaps Christina in the face, punishing her for a previously performed prayer practice (Ch. 28). This behavior of the enlivened sculpture is surprising insofar as this scene follows a description of Mary appearing to Christina in her sleep to heal her injured knees with balm after she had prayed too hard (Ch. 27).[52] Visions of a vindictive Mary, especially in the form of a punishing sculpture, appear predominantly in twelfth- and thirteenth-century miracle stories.[53] In this sense, Christina's case resonates with medieval exempla that were well known during her own lifetime.

Theological reflections on Mary, in particular questions concerning original sin, are also laid out in the *Life.* An allusion to a maculist position is made from Christina's perspective (first-person voice) in the very last part of the *Life* (Ch. 100), which recounts and reflects a vision on the day of Mary's Assumption (August 15): if Mary had died before Christ could have been born, she would have gone straight to limbo, literally to "pre-hell" (*vorhelle*).[54] According to this statement, Mary, though free of sins, had nonetheless automatically attracted original sin. Christina herself is told by Christ that she is confirmed in him "as if it were a fact" that she has never sinned (Ch. 35), implicitly establishing an equivalence on this basis with Mary. Mary's alternative fate in limbo is coherent with the messianic belief that Christ had to be born in order to liberate the souls from hell. Bernard of Clairvaux and early thirteenth-century scholastics, including Bonaventure and Thomas Aquinas, argued that Mary could not have been free of original sin because otherwise she would not have needed salvation. This economy of salvation pertaining to Mary was uniformly believed until the very late thirteenth century, when immaculatist ideas, brought forward by William of Ware and John Duns Scotus, emerged in the British Isles. These arguments, though spreading quickly, could not have reached Christina herself because they only developed around 1290 and it was not until the fourteenth century that they came to the continent, where they then took firmly root.[55] This means that the position held in the *Life* vis-à-vis Mary and original sin is consistent with ideas in Christina's lifetime.

However, considering the Eckhartian elements contained in the *Life* and its late transmission, there might yet exist another historical explanation for the inclusion of the controversial issue of Mary's immaculate or maculate status. Acknowledging that the *Life* was rewritten and augmented in the course of the fourteenth century (and possibly even in the fifteenth), we need to take the late medieval debate on the Immaculate Conception into account, and the position held first and foremost by medieval Dominicans. Following the argumentation of Aquinas, most Dominicans of the late Middle Ages and early Renaissance opposed the idea of the Immaculate Conception, in contrast to Franciscans and the secular clergy.[56] For example, the fourteenth-century Franciscan Marquard of Lindau, a reforming leader of his order and by 1389 provincial minister of the vast area of southern Germany, keenly defended Mary's perfection. Marquard, described by Stephen Mossman as "a very strong candidate to have been the most widely-transmitted medieval German author of all," wrote against those who denied the doctrine of the Immaculate Conception—that is, against Dominicans.[57] Although the Dominicans continuously disapproved of immaculism, the conflict became considerably fiercer in the aftermath of the Council of Basel (1431–1449), when the Immaculate Conception was elevated to a dogma. Dominicans tended to make use of their own saints in their arguments against immaculists, mentioning above all the mystic Catherine of Siena as a maculist.[58] That in *The Life of Christina of Hane* Mary is not free of original sin may hence indicate ties to the fourteenth- and perhaps fifteenth-century Dominican camp, when there existed a heightened sensitivity to this hotly debated issue. The other dispute that divided the orders (in which Marquard of Lindau again defended the Franciscan stance) concerned the primacy of the will or the intellect of the soul.[59] The fact that this debate features prominently in the *Life* makes it even more likely that whoever rewrote the *Life* after Christina's lifetime was interested in important theological questions of their time and was using the hagiographic and mystical text as a vehicle to express their own ideas.

The human-divine similarity between Christina and Mary

is also reflected in the dynamism of the text, where voices constantly shift and where Christ's speech is not always clearly distinguishable from Christina's voice. In one instance the narrator addresses first the "blessed virgin Christina" in a prayerlike appeal and subsequently "our blessed mother" (Ch. 15), leaving it open to interpretation who is meant by the maternal figure, the Virgin Mary or Christina. In this way the allegorical embodiment of the bride of Christ in Christina, configured typologically and in competition with Mary, is also reflected on the text's surface. Christina's special relationship to Christ is further "engraved" into the manuscript matrix: on the opening page of her *Life* as transmitted in the Strasbourg manuscript, the scribe employed an abbreviation for Christ's name, a monogram for the *nomen sacrum,* which is also used for Christina's name here and throughout the text (see fig. 1). The identity between Christ ($\overline{xpm}$) and Christina ($xp\bar{\imath}na$) is thus mirrored on the textual surface and reserved to the mystical couple. This visual strategy of aligning Christ with Christina was a deliberate scribal choice; in contrast, the names of two other figures equally called Christina (or Cristine in an alternative spelling) are fully written out rather than abbreviated with the special monogram. Christina, the *sponsa Christi,* is literally recognizable, and the materiality of her name so intrinsically connected with Christ's name confers a quasi-sacred status to the manuscript.

The reflections expressed from Christina's perspective in the last part of the *Life* take on a scholastic dimension with formulations that refer to the "masters" and ideas borrowed from scientific discourse, in particular from optics. They remain openended as the *Life* ends abruptly in midsentence. That this may well have been a deliberate ending is possible for several reasons.

First, from a codicological point of view, there is no reasonable explanation for why the scribe should have stopped copying their text, as they left considerable space on the page (see fig. 2). Instead they added the abbreviation for "et cetera," further suggesting that this was a considered ending. Second, a dynamic understanding of textuality allows for the fragmentary report to appear performative in its processual open-endedness. The *Life*'s final sentences are about the dying of the soul in God, the liberation from the soul of itself and of any name, and the becoming God of the soul. This process is described as a fluid one. The abrupt ending—"etc."—may thus allude to the ongoing process of the soul becoming God. Third, the *Life* is embedded in a dynamic manuscript culture, one that led to its development over several centuries and secured a continuous engagement with the material. It was not randomly thrown together; the passages between different text parts are fluid, and theological reflections in the latter part of the *Life* are in sync with previously described visions. The open-endedness of the *Life* may therefore be more a sign of the serious, critical, and deliberate involvement of later scribes and recipients, who copied, rewrote, and shaped their material.

This historical condition of a dynamic manuscript culture in which texts are constantly redacted should also help us to revaluate what we may otherwise consider "original mystical theology." Whether the *Life* contains original ideas or reactions to mystical and theological issues does not matter as much as the way it has been composed in a co-creative process over a long period of time. Its versatility shows a mobility of thought where traces of various inspirations are combined with what appear to be new additions to existing debates. The *Life*'s complexity in the kind of mystical theology that it presents—and how it presents it—thus eludes categories of literary genre and gendered experience.

THE MANUSCRIPT: STRASBOURG, BIBLIOTHÈQUE NATIONALE ET UNIVERSITAIRE, MS 324

The only surviving manuscript transmitting the medieval *Life of Christina of Hane* can be found in Strasbourg, Bibliothèque nationale et universitaire, MS 324.[60] The modern title on the book spine specifies the content of the codex as *Statuta sacri et canonici Ordinis Praemonstratensis sub Anno 1505*. The provenance of an old shelf mark (L Lat. 273) on the spine and on fol. 1r cannot be securely determined, but the codex must have been kept at the Premonstratensian Stift in Ilbenstadt until the early nineteenth century. When exactly it arrived at Strasbourg is uncertain; it definitely belonged to the Strasbourg library before 1918, when it was still the (German) Imperial University and State Library as a stamp on the front flyleaf reveals.

A text on the recto side of the front flyleaf specifies that the codex was bound by command of the abbot of Rommersdorf Petrus Diederich in 1662. The same seventeenth-century hand tells us that all of the texts were found in Engelport, a Premonstratensian women's convent that was supervised by the abbot of Sayn, with the exception of the years 1617–1672, when the abbot of Rommersdorf was in charge of the canonesses' supervision.[61] This is the time frame in which Petrus Diederich had access to the books from Engelport.

The Strasbourg codex mainly consists of two distinct parts: the first fascicle contains a recension of the Latin statutes for the Premonstratensian Order from 1505 (fols. 1r–210r); the second fascicle comprises *The Life of Christina of Hane* (fols. 212r–349v) as well as a fragmentary legend about Mary Magdalene's conversion (fols. 350r–355v), both of which are written in a medieval

Mosel Franconian dialect. There is no indication that the two fascicles belonged together before their binding in 1662. Two seventeenth-century hymns by Pieter de Waghenare, a Premonstratensian canon of St. Nicolas in Veurne (Belgium), are copied on the last leaves of the codex: one hymn about Christina of Hane (fols. 356r–358r), the other about Gertrude of Altenberg, abbess of the Premonstratensian convent Altenberg and daughter of St. Elisabeth of Hungary (fols. 358r–359v).

The Latin fascicle is dated to April 22, 1505 (fol. 201r), the date of the decree of the reformed statutes,[62] meaning that the date of the present copy is surely after April 22, 1505. The German fascicle is written on paper that circulated in Europe mostly in the first half of the sixteenth century, but the bastarda script it is written in indicates an earlier time frame: the second fascicle, written in one hand, could have been copied anytime between 1490 and 1530, with a tendency toward the latter half. Based on linguistic observations, *The Life of Christina of Hane* was copied from one or several sources whose composition must have reached back into her lifetime, that is the late thirteenth century. Because some of the theological ideas related to the fourteenth-century mysticism of the Rhineland, it is likely that the *Life* was supplemented over the centuries, before it came down to us in the extant form. For both fascicles, the provenances cannot be fully secured. Given the dialect of the vernacular part, it is possible that the second fascicle was copied in or around Hane.

The Mary Magdalene conversion legend in MS 324 belongs to the transmission of a legend that originated in the Low Countries and first appeared in the fourteenth century as a Latin text attributed to Pseudo-Isidore.[63] The dissemination of this legend in the regions of the Lower Rhine occurred in different languages and dialects including Middle Dutch, Ripuarian, and Middle

Low German in the fifteenth and sixteenth centuries. The late fifteenth-century Mosel Franconian version of the Strasbourg codex stands out as the most southerly witness of this legend.[64]

RECEPTION HISTORY IN THE
EARLY MODERN PERIOD

The convent of Hane was partly destroyed in the course of the Peasants' War in 1525 and completely dissolved in 1564.[65] There is no hard evidence that the *Life* was read in Hane in the late fifteenth or early sixteenth century when the surviving copy was likely produced, but it is possible, as communal life enjoyed a revival under its abbess Margarete of Engelsstadt in the 1540s, after the convent was damaged in the Peasants' War.[66] It is possible that the transmitted copy was of interest at that time, even more so when considering the attention that the Premonstratensian Order experienced in the second half of the sixteenth century—the time of the Counter-Reformation—when its founder, Norbert of Xanten, was celebrated as an ardent devotee of the Holy Host.[67] At a time of political insecurity, it might have been meaningful to transmit the *Life* of Christina as a written memory of the convent and its spiritual tradition. Christina's biography, however individual and bridal-mystical it may be, is embedded in a context of community, recounting events in the convent, habits of specific sisters, and how they took care of Christina's fragile body when it was afflicted by severe diseases. Christina was a figure to whom the last canonesses of Hane might have wanted to relate. Her example would have served as a communal role model, if not one of practical relevance (in relation to spiritual exercises, for example), then certainly one of tradition and identification.

The original late medieval manuscript with Christina's biography (today Strasbourg, BNU, MS 324) was first discovered by Petrus Diederich in 1656. Diederich found the manuscript on a visit to the women's convent of Engelport and, according to his own records, copied it, labeling the manuscript as *antiquissimae vitae libellus*.[68] This copied version, lost today, was sent— with the recommendation to include but abridge Christina's biography—to the Flemish Norbertine Pieter de Waghenare, who at the time was editing a book on Premonstratensian saints. As a result, a Latin hymn of twenty-three strophes was published in Antwerp in 1661.[69]

Though scarcely visible in the manuscript today, an ink younger than that of the main scribe was used in the *Life*'s opening lines to change Christina's convent (see fig. 1). Mittermaier detected the word *Retters* written over the word *Hane* and *Königstein* over *Bolant* and established that this alteration, or rather manipulation, by the hand of a seventeenth-century scribe had occurred in the context of the binding of the manuscript together with Latin statutes for the order in 1662.[70] The codex was kept in Ilbenstadt in the eighteenth century, where Casper Lauer (librarian and later last abbot of the Premonstratensian Stift of Ilbenstadt before its secularization) corrected the word *Bolant* to *Bolandium* and added the geographical specification *versus Cruciniacum in Palatinatu*, meaning near Bad Kreuznach in the Palatinate. This revision back to the original information about Christina's convent, however, was not in the version that had been passed down.

The early modern transmission promoted the thirteenth-century Premonstratensian canoness under a different name, that of "Christina of Retters." Both Premonstratensian convents, Hane near Bolanden and Retters near Königstein, had ceased to exist by the time the manuscript was found in the seventeenth century. Mittermaier implies that Petrus Diederich, abbot of Rommersdorf, was responsible for the alteration of the provenance, since in his letters he only ever referred to "Christina of Retters," whereas someone who had seen the original manuscript would perhaps have noticed the manipulation made under Diederich's watch if not on his command.[71] The reason for altering Christina's convent is still difficult to understand, since both Retters and Hane had been dissolved by the time Petrus made contact with Pieter. A possible explanation is a local interest in Retters, since it used to be a female convent under the supervision of the canons of Rommersdorf.

Diederich was indeed keen to promote Christina's cause. He took up contact with the Bollandists in 1657 and achieved a short entry for Christina in the Acta Sanctorum based on Waghenare's publication.[72] In 1662, a copper print illustrating Christina's prayer for the souls in purgatory appeared in Antwerp but was never circulated (see fig. 3).[73] It shows the mystic in her Premonstratensian habit with a white scapular holding the hand of Christ, who himself carries the cross. Pointing to the souls with her other hand, Christina encourages Christ to turn his attention to the spectacle of souls lifted out of the fire by winged angels. This scene illustrates her supplication to Christ for the souls' liberation. In the upper register of this image we can see the community of saints in heaven, depicted among others as monks, identifiable by their tonsures. The caption of the print (consequently affiliating Christina with Retters) offers a concise summary of what is represented in the illustration: as in the hymn, it is Christina's status as God's chosen bride, her service to the souls in purgatory, and her affiliation to the Premonstratensian Order that are highlighted.

Also in the 1660s, another Flemish canon, Ludolph van Craywinckel, decided to integrate Christina's life story into his own Premonstratensian hagiographic work.[74] A comparison of this 1665 Flemish text with the German original contained in MS 324 reveals significant differences. As a result of stylistic changes, the Flemish adaptation is much more tightly structured. Chapters, which in the German text appear loosely assembled, are regrouped thematically. While the German text is structured according to feast days, the early modern version catalogues Christina's spiritual experiences with corresponding chapter titles, thereby removing its liturgical context. Explanations and additions have been made where necessary to accomplish a coherent narrative with a clear ending. The hagiographic account has been drastically shortened to less than a fifth of the original length. This concentration leads to a shift in how strongly certain topics are emphasized. The medieval German text presents itself as a hagiographic account about mystical encounters, expressed in dialogues, direct auditions, and containing fragmentary text parts that underline the impossibility of speaking about the mystical experience, but the Flemish text evens out these aspects of speculative spirituality. Traces of negative theology and apophatic discourse are suppressed.[75] The mystical union of the soul with Christ, for example, is expressed only covertly and hypothetically in the seventeenth-century text,[76] further suggesting that the union of the wills as brought forward in the *Life* could indeed easily have been read as heretical. Other elements of Christina's biography are given greater prominence, especially those that are removed from theologically divisive questions. Topics more universal to hagiographic texts are emphasized instead—for instance, the cult of saints and prayers for the soul in purgatory. Praying for other souls as part of a mystical life, in particular, presented a form of spirituality that a religious woman could practice within her convent walls.[77] By the seventeenth century, when the Flemish adaptation appeared, the Counter-Reformation flowering of female mysticism had taken on new shapes. The Flemish text shows us how medieval mysticism was readapted to a more acceptable and timely form.

Internal politics within the religious order played an important role in the reception of Christina's case in the seventeenth century. The Premonstratensian Order was traditionally an institution for the nobility; it had flourished during the Middle Ages, but like many other orders it had suffered from a decline in vocations and entire convents had been dissolved following the Reformation. Christina's promotion can be seen as an attempt, albeit a late one, to catch up with modern, more popular orders.[78] On the title-page engraving of Craywinckel's second volume, the Premonstratensian Order is represented as a family, a tree with many branches (see fig. 4). In this version of a Tree of Jesse, St. Norbert rests at the bottom, while the top crown is reserved for Mary as Mother of God. Christina is similarly depicted to her left, alluding to the mystic's special devotion to the infant Jesus. The aspect of order politics becomes particularly marked in the final paragraph of the Flemish text, which emphasizes Christina's affiliation to the White Canons. All members of the order are exhorted to follow her example and keep the white habit, conferred by the Virgin Mary on the founder Norbert, "clean of the stain of sin."[79]

In 1771, Premonstratensian canons published a short Latin version of the *Life* in the form of a note as part of the appendix of a larger compendium on the Order's history.[80] Here, the mystic and visionary is identified as Christina of Retters, perhaps in order to conform with the narrative as it had been established by Petrus Diederich. However, all attempts to promote Christina, who in the sixteenth and seventeenth centuries generally received the epithet "the Blessed," failed or were not further pursued. In the coming centuries, her person and *Life* would sink into oblivion until the oldest extant source, Strasbourg, BNU, MS 324, was rediscovered and finally reevaluated. Following the critical edition from 2017, the present annotated translation into English finally brings Christina and the fascinating *Life* to an Anglophone audience.

NOTE ON TRANSLATION

The present translation is based on the critical edition that I published in a monograph on *The Life of Christina of Hane* in 2017.[81] While the *Life* is not explicitly divided into chapters, breaks between chapters in the edition correspond largely to breaks between paragraphs in the manuscript. The translation adopts the critical edition's chapter structure in order to facilitate referencing the text (chapter numbers appear in italic because they are added), but paragraphs within a chapter are supplemented here as they are meant to assist the reading. Where the manuscript contains a rubricated title I have accepted it as the title of a chapter, appearing in the translation centered below the chapter number. All emendations in the edited text relative to the manuscript are recorded in the apparatus of the critical edition. Such editorial emendations are only noted in the translation when they may affect the meaning of a passage.

Every translation that aims to evoke "the echo of the original" (Walter Benjamin) demands the reader's trust. In this case, the principal purpose of the translation is to make the *Life* more easily available to nonspecialist readers, which means that some ambiguous passages had to be interpreted for the sake of comprehensibility. I have attempted to translate every word in the primary source in order to give an accurate account of the text. As a result, personal pronouns may shift in unintuitive ways as they do in the original text, where these shifts add to a complexity of voices and character configurations (for example, the usual pronoun "it" for the infant Jesus may turn into the male-gendered "he"). When it comes to the pronoun for the soul—gendered "she" in the original—I have decided to use "it," since this helps to differentiate between Christina as speaker and Christina's soul. At some instances, however, even the original is ambiguous, so I have kept the female pronoun "she" in the translation whenever both Christina and her soul could be meant. In regard to common adverbs and conjunctions (especially *unde* and *da*) I have allowed myself some freedom in the translation.

The Life of Christina of Hane is written in medieval Mosel Franconian. This German dialect is closely related to Rhine Franconian and to the well-attested chancellery language of the city of Mainz.[82] Medieval Mosel Franconian is a so-called mixed dialect, meaning that it contains forms of both High and Low German.[83] The *Life* contains several words that are not attested elsewhere. One of these is the noun *kauffen*, which may be an altered form of the Old French *convenance*, also appearing in Neidhart's songs as *govenanz*, meaning a gathering intended for dances and games.[84] At one instance in the *Life*, the (mystical) lover is called *wyne;* relative to the rest of the text, this is an archaic word, which may hint at an early genesis of a text source during Christina's lifetime. While the translation does not represent the archaic tone at this instance, a note indicates the original and its meaning. Latin words in the original text are kept in Latin but appear normalized in the translation, in contrast to some variant spellings in the manuscript.

Certain words in the Mosel Franconian text may be translated in various different ways—for example, the word *andaehtic* may mean "devout," "devotional," "pious," or "contemplative," depending on the context; the word *jnfluße/ynfloiße* can be translated as "stream," "flow," or "infusion"; and *anfechtonge,* meaning "attack" or "struggle," also denotes "adversity." In the case of *vereynionge/vereynigun* we move at the center of mystological questions concerning the soul's union with the divinity; "unification" emphasizes the process, while "union" describes the state achieved. The term *genade,* which is used superfluously in the *Life,* can mean a variety of concepts ranging from divine qualities to human feelings and is therefore notably difficult to translate. I have attempted to distinguish acts of deliverance and clemency (e.g., "mercy," "charity") from a divine state (e.g., "grace") or a human sensation (e.g., "affection"), but there remain a few instances where any of these could apply. In line with medieval German textual convention, the *Life* calls the women of the Premonstratensian convent *jonffrauwen;* while technically these religious women were canonesses, I have decided to mostly translate the term as "nuns" to designate their status as women of the Premonstratensian Order. However, in some cases, especially at the beginning of the *Life, jonffrauwen* can be translated as "virgins," "girls," or more generally "women." Christina is consistently referred to as *jonffrauwe,* which is rendered as "virgin" (and "girl" in a few cases) in the translation, because it is a kind of epithet that highlights her similarity to the Virgin Mary.

The grammar of the *Life* is complex, with long and nested sentences. Inversions of sentences in places, which strike the modern reader as ungrammatical, are common.[85] The translation tries to respect the particularity of the *Life*'s prose whenever possible, while still presenting a readable version of the text. As a consequence, long sentences in the original may appear shorter in the English translation for the sake of comprehensibility. Repetitions of words and word groups in the original are kept in the translation whenever they create intricate rhetorical constructions (for example: *this holy virgin was in fervent devotion as was her habit. As was her habit she was in fervent devotion and desire,* Ch. 23). Next to such chiastic constructions, repeated introit formulas also emulate the language of the Bible; I have decided to introduce a more diverse prose for reasons of intelligibility.

The *Life* uses two words, *kyntheit* and *jogent,* to refer to Christina's childhood; in both cases, what is meant is a spiritual childhood, that is, before Christina's soul is mature to unite with her bridegroom Christ. Hence, the translation renders both words as "childhood" (rather than "youth" for the latter). The word *geist* is translated in its Latinized form, "spirit," compliant with current uses, especially for the Holy Spirit. A variety of words are used to address the mystical companion in terms of a love relationship: the *Life* distinguishes but little between the neutral word *lyebe* ("love"), the active *lyebhaber* ("the one who loves" or "lover"), and the passive *lyebde* ("beloved"). The translation mostly follows these categories—with a few exceptions, where the context allows for more freedom. In any case, even if the "lover" appears in the text, he or she should not be misread as a modern sexual companion, but as the spiritual lover of the bride's or groom's soul.

Missing words and sentences in the *Life* hamper the understanding of the text. Wherever I was forced to add a word or clause to make sense of a passage, I have added a note high-lighting the fragmentary nature of the original phrasing. A number of words in the *Life* are neologisms or uncommon (such as *vbersuße*) which in the translation are mostly rendered with more idiomatic formulations (in this case, "abundantly sweet," "over-sweet," or "sweeter than sweet"). Generally, the *Life* tends toward a hyperbolic use of adjectives, which I have tried to render as close to the original as possible. For grammatical reasons, however, hyperbolic expressions cannot always be translated literally into English—for example, the twofold superlative *aller lyebstes*, which is mostly translated as "very dearest."

The notes in the translation include, as indicated above, critical notes on problematic passages. Furthermore, they function as an apparatus indicating references to Scriptures, other intertextual suggestions, and clarifications on complicated issues. Vulgate quotations are taken from the fifth Stuttgart edition;[86] Psalms are indicated in order of the Vulgate (e.g., Ps 31 corresponds to modern Ps 32); and the books of the Bible are identified by their standard English abbreviations.[87] In the notes, immovable feasts are taken from the medieval calendar of the diocese of Mainz, in which Hane was located. They mostly correspond to current feast days (and if not, I have so indicated). Movable feast days such as Easter and Pentecost are specified with a corresponding calendar date only if the precise year can be determined. Some of Christina's visions that occur on feast days cannot be dated with full certainty; the sequence of feast days delineated in the *Life* contains gaps, which suggests that some text material may have been lost. Supplying exact dates where the year is uncertain would not only superimpose a possibly inaccurate chronology; more importantly, it would strip the reader of an ambiguity and openness concerning the time frame covered by the original. In such cases I have indicated the feast day in relation to a nearby major movable feast, e.g. Easter.

NOTES

1. Kurt Ruh, *Geschichte der abendländischen Mystik*, vol. 2, *Frauenmystik und franziskanische Mystik der Frühneuzeit* (Munich: Beck, 1993), 121.

2. For an extensive study of the text and mystical content of the *Life*, see Racha Kirakosian, ed., *Die Vita der Christina von Hane: Untersuchung und Edition*, Hermaea 144 (Berlin: De Gruyter, 2017) [hereafter cited as Kirakosian, *Die Vita der Christina von Hane*].

3. For a bibliography of primary and secondary sources, see "Further Reading" below.

4. Miri Rubin, *Mother of God: A History of the Virgin Mary* (New Haven, CT: Yale University Press, 2009), 266–267. On Hermann Joseph's bridal mysticism, see Carolyn Diskant Muir, "Bride or Bridegroom? Masculine Identity in Mystic Marriages," in *Holiness and Masculinity in the Middle Ages*, ed. P. H. Cullum and Katherine J. Lewis (Cardiff: University of Wales Press, 2004), 69–73.

5. See Ulrich G. Leinsle, "Zur rechtlichen Ordnung prämonstratensischer Seelsorge im Mittelalter," *Rottenburger Jahrbuch für Kirchengeschichte* 22 (2003): 34; Ingrid Ehlers-Kisseler, "Heiligenverehrung bei den Prämonstratensern: Die Seligen und Heiligen des Prämonstratenserordens im deutschen Sprachraum," *Rottenburger Jahrbuch für Kirchengeschichte* 22 (2003): 77.

6. See Hermann Josef Kugler, *Hermann Josef von Steinfeld (um 1160–1241) im Kontext christlicher Mystik* (St. Ottilien: EOS Verlag, 1992), 58–59, 101–103; Karl Koch and Eduard Hegel, *Die Vita des Prämonstratensers Hermann Joseph von Steinfeld: Ein Beitrag zur Hagiographie und zur Frömmigkeitsgeschichte des Hochmittelalters*, Colonia sacra 3 (Cologne: Balduin Pick, 1958), 101–105.

7. "Norbertines" is the alternative name for the Premonstratensians, called thus after their founder, Norbert of Xanten (c. 1080–1134).

8. The Premonstratensian foundation phase was characterized by the establishing of double monasteries, a practice, however, that quickly grew out of fashion. For an overview of Premonstratensian double monasteries,

see Elsanne Gilomen-Schenkle, "Double Monasteries in the South-Western Empire (1100–1230) and Their Women's Communities in Swiss Regions," in *Partners in Spirit: Women, Men, and Religious Life in Germany, 1100–1500*, ed. Fiona J. Griffiths and Julie Hotchin, Medieval Women: Texts and Contexts 24 (Turnhout, Bel.: Brepols, 2014), 56–61.

9. Franz Paul Mittermaier, "Wo lebte die selige Christina, in Retters oder in Hane?" *Archiv für mittelrheinische Kirchengeschichte* 12 (1960): 92.

10. On the early history of Hane, see Christine Kleinjung, "Die Herren von Bolanden als Klostergründer," *Alzeyer Geschichtsblätter* 33 (2001): 18.

11. We hear of three biological sisters for whom she prays to be liberated from purgatory. The *Life* also mentions a biological brother of Christina who carried the bishop's banner at the Battle of Worringen on June 5, 1288: this would indeed have been the later German king Count Adolf of Nassau (Ch. 23). Another hint regarding her possible family background is Christina's vision of her brother's son and daughter dying at an early age—which, again, was true of Adolf of Nassau's circumstances. For more on Christina's possible family background, see Bruno Krings, "Die Frauenklöster in der Pfalz," *Jahrbuch für westdeutsche Landesgeschichte* 35 (2009): 192; Mittermaier, "Wo lebte die selige Christina," 88. Despite this research, her exact family background remains unclarified; see Kirakosian, *Die Vita der Christina von Hane*, 5–6.

12. See Mechthild von Magdeburg, *Das fließende Licht der Gottheit: Nach der Einsiedler Handschrift in kritischem Vergleich mit der gesamten Überlieferung*, ed. Hans Neumann, vol. 1, *Text*, ed. Gisela Vollmann-Profe, Münchener Texte und Untersuchungen zur deutschen Literatur des Mittelalters 100 (Munich: Artemis, 1990), 2.3.48: *Nu gebristet mir túsches, des latines kann ich nit.*

13. Convent documents indeed testify to a period of poverty in the 1280s. See Mittermaier, "Wo lebte die selige Christina," 79.

14. Thomas de Cantimpré, "Vita Beatae Christina Mirabilis Virginis," in *Acta Sanctorum* [AASS]: *Jul. V [July 24], Julii, ex Latinis & Græcis . . . Tomus V*, ed. Joannes Baptista Sollerius et al. (Antwerp: Jacobus du Moulin, 1727), 650A–660C. English translation by Margot H. King, *The Life of Christina Mirabilis*, Peregrina Translations Series 2 (Toronto: Peregrina, 1989).

15. Wolfram Schneider-Lastin, ed., "Leben und Offenbarung der Elsbeth von Oye: Textkritische Edition der Vita aus dem 'Ötenbacher Schwesternbuch,'" in *Kulturtopographie des deutschsprachigen Südwesten im späteren*

Mittelalter: Studien und Texte, ed. Barbara Fleith and Rene Wetzel, Kulturtopographie des alemannischen Raums 1 (Berlin: De Gruyter, 2009), 395–448.

16. For a study of this self-inflicted penitential program, including Christina's maltreatment of her genitals causing unnatural vaginal bleeding, see Racha Kirakosian, "Penitential Punishment and Purgatory: A Drama of Purification through Pain," in *Punishment and Penitential Practices in Medieval German Writing,* ed. Sarah Bowden and Annette Volfing, King's College London Medieval Studies 26 (London: Boydell & Brewer, 2018), 129–153.

17. I thank Katharine Park for confirming the lack of medieval sources about the female erogenous apparatus.

18. Krings, "Die Frauenklöster in der Pfalz," 193; Franz Paul Mittermaier, "Lebensbeschreibung der sel. Christina, gen. von Retters," *Archiv für mittelrheinische Kirchengeschichte* 18 (1966): 238.

19. Norbert Backmund, *Die mittelalterlichen Geschichtsschreiber des Prämonstratenserordens,* Bibliotheca Analectorum Praemonstratensium 10 (Averbode, Bel.: Praemonstratensia, 1972), 90–91, names a provost called Godebert as hagiographer; Krings, "Die Frauenklöster in der Pfalz," 199–200, identifies as author a provost called Gotsman, who would later become the abbot of Rothenkirchen.

20. On questions of the *Life*'s production, genre, confessor, and literary tradition, see Kirakosian, *Die Vita der Christina von Hane,* 37–71.

21. For a discussion on how bridal mysticism developed as a subset of an Augustinian Neoplatonic tradition, see Bernard McGinn, *The Foundations of Mysticism,* The Presence of God: A History of Western Christian Mysticism 1 (New York: Crossroad, 1991), 108–130.

22. On the development of the motif of the divine heart in the Helfta writings as connected to the feast of Corpus Christi, see Racha Kirakosian, "Das göttliche Herz im 'Fließenden Licht der Gottheit' Mechthilds von Magdeburg: Eine motivgeschichtliche Verortung," *Euphorion* 111 (2017): 257–275. On the development of Corpus Christi, see Miri Rubin, *Corpus Christi: The Eucharist in Late Medieval Culture* (Cambridge: Cambridge University Press, 1991), 58–64; and Thomas Izbicki, *The Eucharist in Medieval Canon Law* (New York: Cambridge University Press, 2015), 101–103.

23. Ruh, *Geschichte der abendländischen Mystik,* 124.

24. The depiction of a celestial celebration of the mass, in which Gertrude partakes, is—like Christina's vision (*Life,* Ch. 33)—filled with descrip-

tions of liturgical sound. For a discussion of Gertrude's visionary *Missa* as a short commentary on the mass, see Jeffrey F. Hamburger et al., *Liturgical Life and Latin Learning at Paradies bei Soest, 1300–1425: Inscription and Illumination in the Choir Books of a North German Dominican Convent* (Münster: Aschendorff, 2016), 1:329, 644–645.

25. See Niklaus Largier, "Medieval Mysticism," in *The Handbook of Religion and Emotion,* ed. John Corrigan (Oxford: Oxford University Press, 2008), 365, 373.

26. For example: *Jch hayn dyr gegeben die clairheit, die myr myn vader hait geben, daz myr vereyniget syn. Myn vader ist yn myr vnd ich yn yme vnd du byst yn vns. Alles das ich hayn, das ist dyne, vnd was du haist, daz ist myn* (*Life,* Ch. 71); *Jch byn yn mym vader vnd du byst yn myr vnd ich yn dyr* (*Life,* Ch. 67). For a discussion of these passages, see Kirakosian, *Die Vita der Christina von Hane,* 186–187.

27. This sort of claim (equality with God) comes close to heresy. Article 21 in the pontifical bull *In agro dominico* (issued by Pope John XXII), which attacks a number of Meister Eckhart's teachings as heretical, criticizes the ambition to become more than the son, that is, the father himself; see Burkhard Hasebrink, "'Mitewürker gotes': Zur Performativität der Umdeutung in den deutschen Schriften Meister Eckharts," in *Literarische und religiöse Kommunikation in Mittelalter und früher Neuzeit: DFG-Symposium 2006,* ed. Peter Strohschneider (Berlin: De Gruyter, 2009), 71.

28. According to Gregory the Great, visions with knowledge about the present-time are as prophetic as predicting visions; see Nigel F. Palmer, "Das Buch als Bedeutungsträger bei Mechthild von Magdeburg," in *Bildhafte Rede in Mittelalter und früher Neuzeit: Probleme ihrer Legitimation und ihrer Funktion,* ed. Wolfgang Harms (Tübingen: M. Niemeyer, 1992), 220.

29. On the so-called Palm Tree Treatise or Latin *Palma contemplationis,* the oldest manuscripts of which date back to the mid-thirteenth century, see Wolfgang Fleischer, *Untersuchungen zur Palmbaumallegorie im Mittelalter,* Münchener Germanistische Beiträge 20 (Munich: Fink, 1976). For a synopsis of its meditative program, see Ruh, *Geschichte der abendländischen Mystik,* 29. The origins of the Latin *Palma contemplationis* lie in Old French; see Wybren F. Scheepsma, *The Limburg Sermons: Preaching in the Medieval Low Countries at the Turn of the Fourteenth Century,* Brill's Series in Church History 34 (Leiden: Brill, 2008), 130; the Old French origins were first asserted by J. Reynaert in "Het vroegste middelnederlandse Palmboomtraktaat," *Ons geestelijk erf* 52 (1978): 296–310.

30. See Jeffrey F. Hamburger, *The Rothschild Canticles: Art and Mysticism in Flanders and the Rhineland circa 1300* (New Haven, CT: Yale University Press, 1990), 2–3; on the image in New Haven, Beinecke, MS 404, fol. 5r—40, see ibid., 35–42.

31. The codex was produced in Saint-Winnoc, possibly for a canoness at the local abbey of Saint-Victor; see Barbara Newman, "Contemplating the Trinity: Text, Image, and the Origins of the Rothschild Canticles," *Gesta* 52 (2013): 133–159. Newman's identification of the provenance means that the speculation on the codex's origins by Wybren F. Scheepsma, "Filling the Blanks: A Middle Dutch Dionysius Quotation and the Origins of the Rothschild Canticles," *Medium Ævum* 70 (2001): 278–303, is outdated.

32. Boethius's influential treatise *De institutione musica* suggests a tripartite understanding of music, through which the human being is connected to the cosmos; see Boethius, "De institutione musica," in *Boetii de institutione arithmetica, libri duo: De institutione musica, libri quinque*, ed. Gottfried Friedlein (Leipzig: Teubner, 1867; reprint Frankfurt: Minerva, 1996), 175–371. On the music of the spheres, see Susan Rankins, "'Naturalis concordia vocum cum planetis': Conceptualizing the Harmony of the Spheres in the Early Middle Ages," in *Citation and Authority in Medieval and Renaissance Musical Culture: Learning from the Learned*, ed. Suzannah Clark and Elizabeth Eva Leach, Studies in Medieval and Renaissance Music 4 (Woodbridge, Suffolk: Boydell Press, 2005), 3–19; Gabriela Ilnitschi, "'Musica mundana': Aristotelian Natural Philosophy, and Ptolemaic Astronomy," *Early Music History* 21 (2002): 37–74. Medieval monastic theory included a fourth aspect: the angels' song (*musica celestis*). In 1415 with Nicolaus de Capua, the *musica mundana* was now also called *musica angelica;* see Oliver Huck, "The Music of the Angels in Fourteenth- and Early Fifteenth-Century Music," *Musica Disciplina* 53 (2003–2008): 99.

33. In this regard, the treatment of the angelic choirs as musical spheres serves as an analogy for Christina's ascent through musical practice; see for example *Life,* Ch. 64.

34. For an analysis of the correlation between musical instances and mystical union in the *Life,* see Racha Kirakosian, "Musical Heaven and Heavenly Music: At the Crossroads of Liturgical Music and Mystical Texts," *Viator* 48 (2017): 121–144.

35. See Eric Palazzo, "Art, Liturgy, and the Five Senses in the Early Middle Ages," *Viator* 40 (2009): 25–56.

36. Augustine, "De Genesi ad litteram XII," in *Patrologia cursus com-*

pletus, omnium ss. patrum, doctorum scriptorumque ecclesiasticorum sive Latino-rum, sive Graecorum. Series Latina, edited by Jacques-Paul Migne, esp. chap. 12, 34:463–464.

37. On the gender-specific implications of Christina's visions and how they are retold in the *Life,* see Kirakosian, *Die Vita der Christina von Hane,* 155–159.

38. It is preceded by her own purging pain on a private penitential level; thus, her own suffering in the light of her "achievements" for the souls in purgatory can be described as proxy pain. See Kirakosian, "Penitential Punishment and Purgatory," 131, 146.

39. The mystic Adelheid Langmann is similarly invested in liberating souls from purgatory, but her numbers do not equal those of Christian of Hane. See Philipp Strauch, ed., *Die Offenbarungen der Adelheid Langmann: Klosterfrau zu Engelthal,* Quellen und Forschungen zur Sprach- und Kultur-geschichte der Germanischen Völker 26 (Strasbourg: K. J. Trübner, 1878), 5, 8, 12, 17, 25, 29, 35, 39, 24.

40. The term "vernacular theology" was introduced by Bernard McGinn: "Meister Eckhart and the Beguines in the Context of Vernacular Theology," in *Meister Eckhart and the Beguine Mystics: Hadewijch of Bra-bant, Mechthild of Magdeburg, and Margerite Porete,* ed. Bernard McGinn (New York: Continuum, 1994), 1–14; McGinn, *The Flowering of Mysticism: Men and Women in the New Mysticism, 1200–1350,* The Presence of God: A History of Western Christian Mysticism 3 (New York: Crossroad Herder, 1998), 19–24. See also Barbara Newman, *God and the Goddesses: Vision, Po-etry, and Belief in the Middle Ages* (Philadelphia: University of Pennsylvania Press, 2003), 295–296; Marleen Cré, *Vernacular Mysticism in the Charterhouse: A Study of London, British Library, MS Additional 37790* (Turnhout, Bel.: Brepols, 2006). Nicholas Watson, who uses the term "vernacular theology" with explicit reference to Bernard McGinn, develops the concept further to emphasize that the vernacular was a platform for an intellectually dynamic culture; see "Censorship and Cultural Change in Late-Medieval England: Vernacular Theology, the Oxford Translation Debate, and Arundel's Con-stitutions of 1409," *Speculum* 70 (1995): 824n4.

41. See Nigel F. Palmer, "The German Prayers in Their Literary and Historical Context," in Jeffrey F. Hamburger and Nigel F. Palmer, *The Prayer Book of Ursula Begerin* (Dietikon-Zurich: Urs Graf Verlag, 2015), 1:382.

42. See Gisilher von Slatheim, "Sermo de Sanctis," in *Paradisus anime intelligentis (Paradis der fornunftigen sele): Aus der Oxforder Handschrift Cod.*

Laud. Misc. 479 nach E. Sievers Abschrift, ed. Philipp Strauch, Deutsche Texte des Mittelalters 30 (Berlin: Weidmann, 1919; reprint Hildesheim: Weidmann, 1998), 90–92; Meister Eckhart, "Predigt Q 70," in Meister Eckhart, *Die deutschen und lateinischen Werke: Die deutschen Werke,* vol. 3, ed. Josef Quint (Stuttgart: W. Kohlhammer, 1976), 188. For this debate in Ruusbroec's writings, see Geert Warnar, "Men of Letters: Medieval Dutch Literature and Learning," in *University, Council, City: Intellectual Culture on the Rhine, 1300–1550: Acts of the XIIth International Colloquium of the Société Internationale pour l'Étude de la Philosophie Médiévale, Freiburg im Breisgau, 27–29 October 2004,* ed. Laurent Cesalli, Nadja Germann, and Maarten J. F. M. Hoenen (Turnhout, Bel.: Brepols, 2007), 243–444.

43. For a full analysis of this question in relation to the scholastic tradition, see Racha Kirakosian, "Which Is the Greatest—Knowledge, Love, or Enjoyment of God? A Comparison between Christina of Hane and Meister Eckhart," *Medieval Mystical Theology* 23 (2014): 20–33.

44. See especially Meister Eckhart's *Talks of Instruction* and *On Detachment,* both in Meister Eckhart, *Die deutschen und lateinischen Werke: Die deutsche Werke,* vol. 5, *Meister Eckharts Traktate,* ed. Josef Quint (Stuttgart: W. Kohlhammer, 1963; reprint 1987). See also Kirakosian, *Die Vita der Christina von Hane,* 95–98.

45. Barbara Newman, "Book Review: Racha Kirakosian, *Die Vita der Christina von Hane: Untersuchung und Edition,*" *Speculum* 94 (2019): 234.

46. Kurt Köster, "Christina von Hane (Hagen), gen. Retters," in *Die deutsche Literatur des Mittelalters: Verfasserlexikon: Begründet von Wolfgang Stammler, fortgeführt von Karl Langosch,* 2nd ed., ed. Kurt Ruh et al. (Berlin: De Gruyter, 1978), 1:1227.

47. The *Liber Positionum* quotes Eckhart directly; it can be found in Franz Pfeiffer, *Deutsche Mystiker des vierzehnten Jahrhunderts,* vol. 2, *Meister Eckhart* (Leipzig: G. J. Göschen, 1857), 628–684. The passage reverberating with Ch. 78 of the *Life* is on p. 678 (n. 148). For a description of the *Liber Positionum* in context of its reception history, see Dagmar Gottschall, "Eckhart and the Vernacular Tradition: Pseudo-Eckhart and Eckhart Legends," in *A Companion to Meister Eckhart,* ed. Jeremiah Hackett, Brill's Companions to the Christian Tradition 36 (Leiden; Brill, 2013), 509–551.

48. Meister Eckhart, "Predigt 77," in *Die deutschen Werke* 3:330–346.

49. Intertexts—apart from the Scriptures and later mystical texts—might have included medieval German Marian poems, a Hester poem of the Teutonic Order (*Deutschordensdichtung*), and the German *Brandan;* see

Kirakosian, *Die Vita der Christina von Hane,* 72–86, 198–235.

50. The idea of Christina being led into the angelic choirs reverberates with Alan of Lille's *Anticlaudianus,* where deified souls are awarded with unequal degrees of gifts but with equal joy; see Alan of Lille, "Anticlaudianus," in *Literary Works,* ed. and trans. Winthrop Wetherbee, Dumbarton Oaks Medieval Library 22 (Cambridge, MA: Harvard University Press, 2013), 5.443–470. The comparison to Alan's *Anticlaudianus* underscores Christina's role as Queen of Heaven; in the twelfth-century poem, for example, we read about the Virgin (Mary) whose dignity surpasses that of everyone else (ibid., 5.471–473). Also, Christina's crown with twelve gems shining like twelve stars (*Life,* Ch. 63) echoes not only many other religious texts (see Kirakosian, *Die Vita der Christina von Hane,* 215–216), but it may also be related to the diadem of Theology in Alan's *Anticlaudianus* (5.101–103).

51. In the *Life,* the *sedes sapientiae* motive and the seven wisdoms are unrelated to the medieval *Artes Liberales* tradition (despite Mary traditionally being matron of the Liberal Arts). On Mary and the Liberal Arts, see Michael Stolz, "Maria und die Artes liberales: Aspekte einer mittelalterlichen Zuordnung," in *Maria in der Welt: Marienverehrung im Kontext der Sozialgeschichte 10.–18. Jahrhundert,* ed. Claudia Opitz et al., Clio Lucernensis 2 (Zurich: Chronos, 1993), 95–120.

52. For an analysis of Marian visions in the *Life* and how they relate to liturgical space, see Racha Kirakosian, "La vision spirituelle dans l'espace corporel et le pouvoir performatif du langage dans la biographie mystique de Christina de Hane," *Le Moyen Âge* 123 (2017): 589–607.

53. For example, a twelfth-century miracle at Canterbury as recounted by Gerald of Wales, "Gemma ecclesiastica, distinction," in *Giraldi Cambrensis opera,* ed. J. S. Brewer (London: Longman, 1869), 2:105–107. For a discussion, see Jean-Marie Sansterre, "'Omnes qui coram hac imagine genua exerint . . .': La vénération d'images de saints et de la Vierge d'après les textes écrits en Angleterre du milieu du xie aux premières décennies du xiiie siècle," *Cahiers de civilisation médiévale* 49 (2006): 278. See also Alexa Sand, "Vindictive Virgins: Animate Images and Theories of Art in Some Thirteenth-Century Miracle Stories," *Word & Image: A Journal of Verbal/Visual Enquiry* 26 (2010): 150–159.

54. On the handling of the afterlife and the resurrection of the body in German-language texts, see Timothy R. Jackson, "Versehrtheit, Unversehrtheit und der auferstandene Körper," in *Verletzungen und Unversehrtheit in der deutschen Literatur des Mittelalters: XXIV. Anglo-German Colloquium,*

Saarbrücken 2015, ed. Sarah Bowden, Nine Miedema, and Stephen Moss-man (Tübingen: Narr Dr. Gunter, 2020), 141–154.

55. Marielle Lamy, *L'immaculée conception: Étapes et enjeux d'une contro-verse au Moyen-Âge, XIIe–XVe siècles,* Collection des études augustiniennes: Série Moyen-Âge et temps modernes 35 (Paris: Institut d'études augustini-ennes, 2000), 396–408.

56. Ulrich Horst, *Die Diskussion um die Immaculata Conceptio im Domi-nikanerorden: Ein Beitrag zur Geschichte der theologischen Methode,* Veröffent-lichungen des Grabmann-Institutes zur Erforschung der Mittelalterlichen Theologie und Philosophie, n.F. 34 (Paderborn: F. Schöningh, 1987), 7–11; and Lamy, *L'immaculée conception,* 422–430.

57. Stephen Mossman, "The Western Understanding of Islamic The-ology in the Later Middle Ages: Mendicant Responses to Islam from Ric-coldo da Monte di Croce to Marquard von Lindau," *Recherches de théologie et philosophie médiévales* 74 (2007): 171.

58. For a detailed study on this debate, see Thomas M. Izbicki, "The Immaculate Conception and Ecclesiastical Politics from the Council of Ba-sel to the Council of Trent: The Dominicans and Their Foes," *Archiv für Reformationsgeschichte* 96 (2005): 145–170. "Dominican Maculism did not vanish overnight," but Pope Sixtus IV's (1471–1484) decrees weakened the opposition; ibid., 169.

59. Mossman, "The Western Understanding of Islamic Theology," 172–173.

60. For a full description of the manuscript, see Kirakosian, *Die Vita der Christina von Hane,* 259–275.

61. On the history of Engelport, see the publication series Norbert J. Pies and Werner P. Pfeil, eds., *Zur Geschichte von Kloster Maria Engelport,* 13 vols. (Erftstadt: Pies & Pfeil, 1989–2000).

62. See Emile Valvekens, "Le chapitre général de Prémontré et les nou-veaux statuts de 1505," *Analecta Praemonstratensia* 14 (1938): 83–84.

63. For a synoptic view of all text witnesses and their translations, see the project website *Exploring Medieval Mary Madgalene,* http://digital-editing.fas.harvard.edu.

64. See Kirakosian, *Die Vita der Christina von Hane,* 281–282. The edi-tion of the Mary Magdalene legend as it is transmitted in Strasbourg, Bib-liothèque nationale et universitaire, MS 324, can be found ibid., 347–349.

65. For the history of Hane (Latin, Hagen), see Norbert Backmund, *Monasticon Praemonstratense: Id est historia circariarum et canoniarum candidi*

et canonici Ordinis Praemonstratensis (Berlin: De Gruyter, 1983), 1:96–98.

66. See Backmund, *Die mittelalterlichen Geschichtsschreiber,* 97.

67. See Manfred Heim, "Prämonstratenser," in *Mönchtum, Orden, Klöster: Von den Anfängen bis zur Gegenwart: Ein Lexikon,* 2nd ed., ed. Georg Schwaiger (Munich: Beck, 1994), 358.

68. See Kurt Köster, "Leben und Gesichte der Christina von Retters (1269 bis 1291)," *Archiv für mittelrheinische Kirchengeschichte* 8 (1956): 242.

69. The whole hymn is reprinted in Franz Paul Mittermaier, "Ein bislang verschollener Hymnus (v. Pieter de Waghenare) auf die sel. Christina, gen. von Retters," *Archiv für mittelrheinische Kirchengeschichte* 10 (1958): 353–355.

70. Many early modern annotations were made in the manuscript's margins. For a list of all hands appearing in the manuscript, see Mittermaier, "Lebensbeschreibung der sel. Christina," (1965): 216.

71. See Franz Paul Mittermaier, "Das Verhältnis des Altenberger Priors Petrus Diederich (1643–1655) zu den Prämonstratenserstiften Ober- und Nieder-Ilbenstadt in der Wetterau," *Wetterauer Geschichtsblätter* 7/8 (1959): 117–131.

72. Joannes Pinius, ed., "Commentarius Praevus: Christina virgo, cognomento Mirabilis, Trudonopoli in Belgio (S.)," III, in *Acta Sanctorum* [AASS], *Jul. V [July 24], Julii, ex Latinis & Græcis . . . Tomus V,* ed. Joannes Baptista Sollerius et al. (Antwerp: Jacobus du Moulin, 1727), 641D: *Inter Præmonstratenses S. Christinam nostram ponit Petrus de Waghenare in suo S. Norberto prosaico, pag. 145.*

73. The only extant print made by the engraver Frans Huybrechts (1650–1687) was put into a manuscript volume with the title *Antiquitates monasterii Aldenburgensis* (p. 711), which is kept at the family archives of Count Solms-Braunfels in Braunfels; see fig. 3. Petrus Diederich collected various materials concerning the order that he put together in this volume, which carries the title of the Premonstratensian convent of Altenberg. He also documented the intended caption for the print (p. 478). The copperplate might therefore have been a test version, which was then never used for printing more copies. The extant print was reproduced in original size in Köster, "Leben und Gesichte der Christina von Retters," 250. Huybrechts was a prolific engraver and repeatedly depicted motives related to the Norbertines; see for example Norbert of Xanten as archbishop (of Magdeburg) in Paris, Bibliothèque nationale de France, Département des estampes et de la photographie, SNR-1 (HUBERTI, François); Amster-

dam, Rijksmuseum, RP-P-OB-33.233, RP-D-2014-9-4, and RP-P-BI-5925 (the same print also London, British Musem, 1891,0414.1095).

74. Ludolphus van Craywinckel, "Het leven vande salighe maghet Christina," in *Legende der levens ende gedenck-weerdige daden van de voornaemste Heylige . . . in de witte orden van den H. Norbertus* (Antwerp: Gerard Wolsschat, 1665), 2:730–759. Christina's biography is preceded by a short history of her alleged convent Retters.

75. For a comparison between the accounts, see Racha Kirakosian, "Rhetorics of Sanctity: Christina of Hane in the Early Modern Period—with a Comparison to a Mary Magdalene Legend," *Oxford German Studies* 43, no. 4 (December 2014): 383–389.

76. Craywinckel, "Het leven," chap. 15, 747: *Het is nochtans waerschijnelijck dat sy ghelijck wierdt aenhaeren Bruydegom.* The author assumes that one identity of Christina's soul and Christ was "probable," whereas the German text repeatedly evokes the union of the wills as well as the unification of Christ and soul.

77. This is the more relevant considering late medieval reform movements that brought enclosure to nunneries and women's convents; on the practice of enclosure, see Heike Uffmann, "Inside and Outside the Convent Walls: The Norm and Practice of Enclosure in the Reformed Nunneries of Late Medieval Germany," *Medieval History Journal* 4 (2001): 83–108.

78. See John Patrick Donnelly, SJ, "New Religious Orders for Men," in *Reform and Expansion 1500–1600*, ed. Ronnie Po-chia Hsia, The Cambridge History of Christianity 6 (Cambridge: Cambridge University Press, 2007), 162: "Some older orders [. . .] virtually disappeared" while the "period saw the creation of new male and female orders and congregations that reshaped Catholicism in the next 500 years."

79. See Craywinckel, "Het leven," chap. 24, 759.

80. Caspar Lauer, "Vita beatae Christinae," in *Spiritus literarius Norbertinus a scabiosis Casimiri Oudini calumniis vindicatur seu sylloge viros ex ordine Praemonstratensi*, ed. Georg Lienhard (Augsburg: Matthäus Rieger, 1771), 597–602.

81. Kirakosian, *Die Vita der Christina von Hane*, 283–349. N.B. In what follows, the primary source is cited simply as *Vita*, whereas the analytical part of my 2017 monograph is referenced as Kirakosian, *Die Vita der Christina von Hane*.

82. Rudolf Schützeichel, *Mundart, Urkundensprache und Schriftsprache: Studien zur Sprachgeschichte am Mittelrhein*, Rheinisches Archiv 54 (Bonn: Röhrscheid, 1960).

83. For characteristics of the Rhine-Franconian dialect, see Nigel F. Palmer, "'In kaffin in got': Zur Rezeption des 'Paradisus anime intelligentis' in der Oxforder Handschrift MS. Laud. Misc. 479," in *"Paradisus anime intelligentis": Studien zu einer dominikanischen Predigtsammlung aus dem Umkreis Meister Eckharts,* ed. Burkhard Hasebrink et al. (Tübingen: Niemeyer, 2009), 102–104. See also Theodor Frings, *Mittelfränkisch-niederfränkische Studien,* vol. 1, *Das ripuarisch-niederfränkische Übergangsgebiet,* Beiträge zur Geschichte der deutschen Sprache und Literatur 41 (Halle: Niemeyer, 1917); Roland Martin, *Untersuchungen zur rhein-moselfränkischen Dialektgrenze,* Deutsche Dialektgeographie 11a (Marburg: N. G. Elwert, 1922).

84. For example, *Neidhart-Lieder: Texte und Melodien sämtlicher Handschriften und Drucke,* vol. 1, ed. Ulrich Miller et al. (Berlin: De Gruyter, 2007), songs 10, 11, here song 35: *in der stuben uber al, / daz die iungen niht verdriesse. / da'z dem meier ist der schal, / da hoeret man den govenanz. / Chuonzel, Heinzel, lat da schowen, / daz mit ziuhten ge der tanz.*

85. For a comprehensive overview of the *Life*'s language including consonants, vowels, morphology, syntax, and lexis, see Kirakosian, *Die Vita der Christina von Hane,* 268–273.

86. Bonifatius Fischer, Robert Weber, and Roger Gryson, eds., *Biblia sacra: Iuxta Vulgatam versionem,* 5th ed. (Stuttgart: Deutsche Bibelgesellschaft, 2007).

87. Chr = Chronicles; Est = Esther; Ez = Ezekiel; Jn = John; Kgs = Kings; Lk = Luke; Mt = Matthew; Prv = Proverbs; Ps = Psalm(s); Rev = Revelation; Rom = Romans; Sg = Song of Songs; Tb = Tobit; Thes = Thessalonians; Ws = Wisdom (of Solomon).

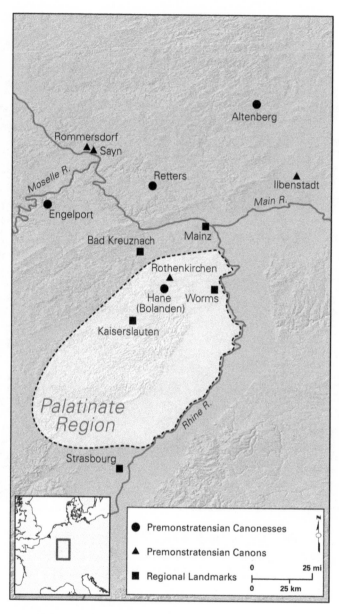

Regional map with landmarks and relevant convents.
Map created by C. Scott Walker, Digital Cartography
Specialist, Harvard Map Collection

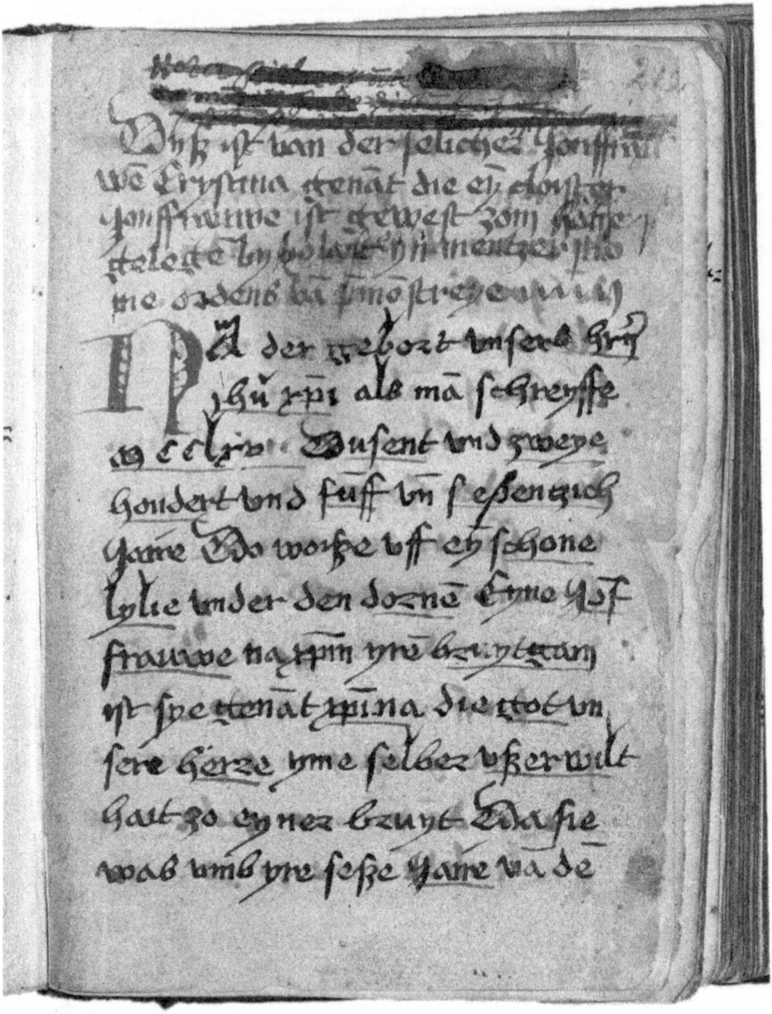

Fig. 1. Opening page of *The Life of Christina of Hane.*
Strasbourg, Bibliothèque nationale et universitaire, MS 324,
fol. 212r. Photo & collection BNU Strasbourg

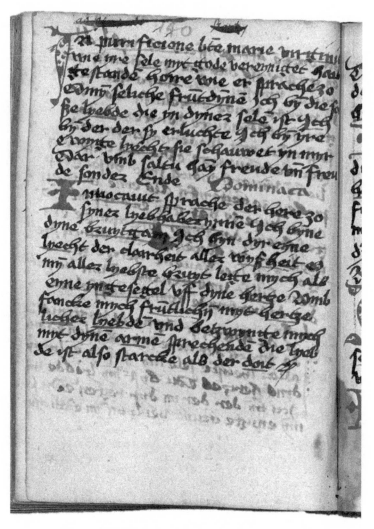

Fig. 2. Empty lines in *The Life of Christina of Hane*
indicating irregularity of scribal behavior. Strasbourg,
Bibliothèque nationale et universitaire, MS 324, fol. 28rv.
Photo & collection BNU Strasbourg

B. CHRISTINA à CHRISTO, qui eam in Sponsam elegerat, sic dicta,
Monasterij Rhetersensis in Dioecesi Moguntina, ordinis Praem. Monialis
postquam visionibus, ecstasibus, illustrationibus, vaticinijs, varijsq; alijs
divinis favoribus cumulata, in coeli è purgatorio tria animarum millia educ
impetriasset à Sponso, ab eodem in coelum è mundo et ipsa educta est an 1291
R̃.D.ae Norbertae Prevost Priorissae Bethaniensi, caeterisq; Furnis
ejusdem loci Norbertinis Virginibus F.P.D. W.D.C.Q.
Franc. Huber.

Fig. 3. Copper print "Beata Christina a Christo"
by Frans Huybrechts (Antwerp, 1662)—*Antiquitates
monasterii Aldenburgensis*, p. 711. Manuscript held at the
Archives of Count von Oppersdorff Solms-Braunfels
in Braunfels. Reproduction: Markus Hurt, Archivist

Fig. 4. Title page of Ludolphus van Craywinckel,
Legende der levens ende gedenck-weerdige daden van de
voornaemste Heylige . . . in de witte orden can den H. Norbertus,
vol. 2 (Antwerp: Gerard Wolsschat, 1665), fol. 1r.
Reproduction: Stadsarchief Mechelen, M.05271(a)/II

THE LIFE OF CHRISTINA OF HANE

This book is about a blessed virgin named Christina
who was a nun in the Premonstratensian convent of Hane,
near Bolanden, in the diocese of Mainz.[1]

I

In the year of our Lord Jesus Christ 1275 a beautiful lily grew among thorns. She was a virgin named Christina—after Christ her bridegroom—whom God our Lord himself chose to be his bride. When she was about six years old, her family gave her to a convent on God's, her bridegroom's, advice to join other good virgins wearing white gowns. Among them she shone like a rose among other flowers. She is truly a second Esther, who was raised for the real Xerxes among other virgins, and was kept in the house called the virgins' house so as to be adorned with perfect virtues and to be joined to him in a high and sacred love. In the same way we read that Lady Esther was most beautiful and lovely and fully pleasing. When she was led before the king, he took a great liking to her, and he loved her—as we find written—more than any other woman. She received more mercy and charity from him than any of her peers, so that she alone was crowned by him. He also brought peace to his entire country and distributed great royal gifts to all his subjects when he took her as a bride.[1] All this is spiritually renewed in this virgin.

Ah, how very pleasing she is before the eyes of the eternal King! Oh, how very worthily he has crowned her before all of us! Oh, how often has he granted peace and mercy to this entire country through her, because he has consummated his marriage to her soul in true union, forever!

2

Now I shall return to the narrative.[1] After she had entered the convent she joined the school at the age of ten, according to the custom of the order. During that year and in the subsequent year she always strove to be alone because her young and tender soul recognized through its nobility that her bridegroom was very coy and would not kiss her until he had given her the jewel of divine love. Whenever she was not otherwise able to withdraw from other children, she hid from her playmates, attempting thereby to abandon childish ways so that her wise heart[2] could, in steadfast contemplation, consider the childhood of our dear Lord. This virgin at times contemplated what a beautiful and lovely child Jesus was; how lovingly he played with the other children; how the mighty God, who clothes all the angels with his light, lay as a small child wrapped up in poor linen in the manger; and how he, who has sealed all wisdom in himself, lay as a child in the cradle by his mother in Nazareth. The virgin carried this contemplation incessantly in her heart.

Ah, how very often she so lovingly and amicably took the child with true desire into the arms of her soul! Oh, how very often she bathed it devoutly with tears of her heart! Oh, how often with pious devotion she named him in her soul and sang to him silently, for it pleases the Infant to be fondled and tenderly embraced, as one is able to play with him lovingly.

3

At one time in those days her heart's contemplation was so assiduously set on the lovely infant Jesus that, standing in the choir with the other women, she saw the most beautiful infant that her heart could long for: the infant was in the sun, which shone through a window into the choir. This was Jesus, the loveliest child of the Holy Virgin Mary. The child played with the sun in front of her as if he wanted to build himself a bed out of sun. In this way he made her understand that he would only rest in a heart as pure as the sun. Later she turned all her diligence toward purifying her heart with perfect light, as you will find written below.

Once the child had played for a while with the sun in front of her, it got up, and walked toward her, and stepped straight ahead until it had reached her, and then it slipped under her virginal cloak. At this her heart was filled with joy. But when she wanted to grasp him in joyful desire to embrace, hold, and kiss, and tenderly press to her heart the loveliest child, she did not find him, because he had disappeared from her just as he had disappeared from the disciples in Emmaus, as the Gospel says.[1]

Oh, how very well she was then able to say with loving and deep sighs, "Was not my heart on fire because of Jesus whom I have seen, whom I love?"[2] From this moment on her great joy was turned into sweet sorrow, fueling her great desire in such a way that she immediately began to cry inwardly, with great lamenting and longing, for the most beautiful infant Jesus.

4

At another instance in those days she began to consider her heart not pure enough to be spiritually inhabited by the lovely infant Jesus, although in truth her sins were very few, for she had been a chaste and pure six-year-old virgin when her parents had brought her to the other chaste virgins in the convent. Nevertheless she lamented her sins heavily in her heart because he who is just judges himself.[1] Therefore she directed all her thoughts to how she would confess absolutely all her sins to her abbot in order to purify her heart from all the dust of sin once and for all. She carried this idea and the grief over her sins constantly in her heart.

One day, during mass, as she sat down in her choir stall with such thoughts in her mind, our dear Lord poured the grace of a complete rest over her so that her heart and her eyes flowed into one another in a sweet ardent cry. She stopped the weeping as she saw our Lord in the priest's hands in the shape of the loveliest infant, at which her senses were suddenly enraptured and her heart was in unmeasurable joy, and her heart and soul were kindled by the love of the tender and beautiful child, and she was impatiently awaiting the moment that she should behold her heart's joy. Promptly the child disappeared from her sight, and thus her joy was turned into deep sorrow. But the loyal God, who is the only comforter for those who long for him, comforted her so amicably with himself, whom she had desired from all her heart.

Once she heard a voice speaking spiritually and inwardly.[2] It was our Lord saying to her soul, "My child, this vision[3] shall be a true testimony to you that all the sins you have ever committed are forgiven." Thenceforth her heart was as pure as the sun, in which the lovely infant had symbolically played in the choir.

As the Prophet says in the Psalter, "Our dear Lord has built his house, which is his dwelling place, in the sun."[4] This means that he only wants to be in a heart that is as pure as the sun.

Oh, how he has built and planted a delightful and constant dwelling place in the sun of this chaste virgin's pure heart, as you will very often find written below.

5

On the Feast Day Nativitatis Domini[1]

In the same year, when the feast day of our Lord's birth was approaching, celebrating that the lovely infant Jesus was born, this blessed virgin unceasingly turned all her desire, thoughts, and contemplation to the dear infant. The childhood of Jesus increased her desire; moreover, the present feast of the divine Virgin-born infant's nativity kindled in her the desire to prepare herself for the dear child: if the Infant found her heart and soul worthy enough for him to be spiritually born in her, then she would be able to enjoy the dear child to her heart's desire.

Thus she stayed awake all night on Christmas Eve, locked up alone in the choir overnight. A perfect heart may notice now that her love and her longing for the dear infant were so great that love overpowered her: although she was a young little girl and furthermore naturally frail, she did not fear being locked up alone in a church for a long dark night. Just as Mary Magdalene found Jesus her Lord, whom she loved, by the grave,[2] so this lonesome virgin found the dear infant Jesus, whom she loved, in the choir. She had ardently yearned to find him. She told me herself that she had prayed a dozen times fifty Paternosters, and that she had exhausted and wearied herself with genuflection, prayer, and desire, until her natural strength failed and she could neither pray nor desire any more.

Then a rapture came upon her spirit. During this rapture she saw in a spiritual vision that the most lovely infant Jesus was walking up in front of her to play in the choir stalls, and he was treading on the most beautiful roses that there have ever been. These were no earthly roses; they were heavenly. The heavenly child played in these roses in front of the virgin, signifying to her what her life would be like, as though he said, "Only a clean heart without the stains of sin and as pure as the sun is enough for me to dwell in. For it must be clean and it must also be adorned with heavenly roses, that is, with all the virtues."

With full diligence and firm exercises she set herself to gain all the virtues, as you will find written below.

6

Now I shall return again to the narrative. The vision of the lovely infant filled her heart and soul with joy, sweetness, and comfort. When the bell for matins was rung, and the women set off to celebrate the Infant's birth, she joined them in their song with great jubilation and with great joy in her heart. In front of the altar she saw the gentle and most beautiful child lying in a cradle, covered with a blanket of roses. On each rose petal the word "Paternoster" was written. A wreath of twelve very handsome roses was wrapped around his head. God gave her to understand that these were the twelvefold fifty Paternosters that she had said for the infant Jesus. At the sight of the dear infant she desired that he would come near to her. Instantly he started off and walked until he reached her. As he stood in front of her in the choir stalls he grew so tall that he became a handsome young man, tall enough to have his head reach her mouth.

This was a sign that God the Lord intended to grow henceforth in her heart and elevate her through his childhood to a high love. If you are willing to read this booklet with all the diligence of your heart, you will be able to note how God elevated her from one thing to the other through his divine wisdom.

While the child was growing in front of her and with her as I have described,[1] it joined her in whatever she was singing and reading. Oh, joyful jubilation! Ah, how joyfully her heart and soul were eager to sing! As she was about to sing the sixth responsory, she saw the gentle infant sitting on the book, singing with her so that she sang into his mouth, and he into hers. I deem that no tongue can tell the sweetness, comfort, and delight that her noble soul then experienced. Her heart and her eyes overflowed into a sweet and dear weeping because of this righteous, gentle, and indulgent delight. Her weeping lasted throughout the whole mass.

7

Our Lord regularly granted this blessed virgin the blessing and benediction of his grace. Starting from the young age of six, when she was given to the convent, God granted more grace to her than to the others while she was still a child, that she devotedly honor our Lord's wounds with genuflection and prayer, whenever she saw them painted or drawn.

There was one particular crucifix that stood in the dormitory, that is, the place which is also called the sleeping hall. She told me herself that whenever she went to that crucifix, she was never so happy as when she fell to her knees in front of it, thanking our

Lord for the sorrowful death that he had suffered on the cross for humankind. Quite often when she went there, she thought in great devotion, "Ah, here is my lover and he waits for me; and he has stretched his arms towards me in order to embrace me with his arms and draw me to him." With such thoughts she opened her arms, and with great longing and devotion in her heart she said, "Hail, Holy Cross, you are the only promise of our salvation!" She fell down to her knees with arms outstretched and lay in front of the crucifix in her prostration for a long time, even though her magistra[1] often punished her severely—and sometimes even beat her—for having stayed too long at her prayer in front of the cross. But punishment and blows, anything that made her suffer, appeared sweet to her because of him who had suffered great pain for her upon the cross. Instead of abandoning her prayer practice, she wanted to persist for the divine grace granted to her by God.

One time it so happened that as she stood in prayer in front of the cross she saw a very handsome white dove fly out of the mouth of the crucifix. The dove flew across the dormitory (or sleeping hall) and turned toward her to circle her head, and touch her head and mouth with its wings. When she tried to catch the dove she heard a voice coming from the dove saying, "Human, go your way without fear and be glad. The Holy Spirit is in you and above you and with you." Then both the voice and the dove vanished simultaneously. The dove is the same Holy Spirit who in the shape of a dove had hovered above our Lord when he was baptized by Saint John, as one reads in the Gospel.[2] The same dove now flew above this virgin, his bride, as if to make her heart and soul a dwelling place and temple for the Holy Spirit, strong and steady in great suffering, as you will hear later. The dove floated above her as if the Holy Spirit wanted to show that she should follow it and float above herself. No heart can tell how high and how far she then flew above herself in high contemplation, unless it had flown with her soul into God. Yet I shall describe but a portion of this, as if I extracted a drop from the sea. The dove, which was sent to her, also crossed the entire sleeping hall of the sisters. This I take to signify that the Holy Spirit was sent to sanctify the entire community through her merits.

8

I will also not remain silent about the magnanimous grace that God granted her when she was in rapture: God gave her the light of knowledge which made her recognize him in all living beings. As a lesson for others, and so that a simple person may better understand, I will explain some things I have heard directly from her.

Whenever she managed to withdraw herself from her peers, who were with her at school, she deeply desired to be completely alone. In such moments she would feed her soul with holy thoughts, because when she was alone she was able to find God in all living beings. While she stood alone by the well she saw how the drinking vat overflowed with water, and she thought of how the abundantly sweet godhead overflows into his angels and saints in heaven and down here to earth. With great desire she begged our dear Lord to flow into her soul with his mercy. Whenever she was in the garden, and saw the earth adorned with flowers and grass, she received great joy, similar to the saint King David, who always received the Holy Spirit upon entering his garden. In the same way, this holy virgin considered how God, who had delicately and multifariously clothed the earth, is beautiful and gracious and uplifting in himself. With great desire she then begged our dear Lord to make her heart blossom with spiritual flowers of virtue. At times this thought came upon the holy virgin when she stood in the cloister with the other women; she would then not be able to join the others in praying the office for the dead. Also, whenever she saw trees reaching high up into the sky she found God, and she begged him to turn and orient her heart toward him with steadfast love and high knowledge. Also, sometimes when sitting alone by the brook and watching the water flow away, she would think, "All things I have done in vain have flowed away like this water, and they shall never return." At this she started to cry with great grief, lamenting to God with fervent tears that she had not spent all her days seeking him in all diligence.

Well, to cut this short: she found God in all things. All her senses, namely seeing and hearing, drew God from all creatures and filled her heart with him and joined him to her soul. Oh, diligent reader, now you have heard how this blessed virgin Christina spent her childhood, her school years. Letters were not everything she learned; she was also educated to lead a spiritual life. Enough has been said now about her childhood and about what happened to her when she was young.

9

The year after she had finished school all the girls had to be sent away from the convent because it was too poor. Each one was sent to her parents and relatives, this girl included.[1] Now you will hear how very diligently she endeavored to adorn her heart with virtues. Once she had realized that God would only dwell

among the flowers of a virtuous heart, she turned all her diligence to making her heart flourish with perfect virtues. But the
meanest Foe, who is against all virtue, turned all his diligence to
stopping her and defeating her with vices. Just as Saint Gregory
wrote, "The more someone strives for heaven, the more the Foe
attacks him and the more vehemently he fights him."[2] About
this fight—how long and how variously the Enemy challenged
her with vices, in particular with the seven mortal sins—you are
now going to hear.

I also want to take this opportunity to describe in part how
wisely she withstood all vices with strict exercises, how she
overcame all of them and trod them down. Thus she became a
paragon[3] and an example to all those who face a battle against
the attacks of the vices. I have never read about anyone who has
fought so hard and in so many ways against adversity, and who
has brought themselves into such danger to fully overcome it.
We may well read about sundry saints who struggled zealously
against many vices and who overcame them perfectly. Likewise,
many pious people on earth still struggle individually with numerous adversities—adversities that they can defeat with God's
help. In contrast, this holy virgin Christina did not simply fight
a few, say two or three; neither did she fight for one or two years.
No, she fought for seven whole years against the seven cardinal
sins, for a full year against each one, until they were altogether
perfectly overcome; and I shall now write some things about this.

10

So this holy virgin was sent to her relatives, as you have heard
before, and spent half a year in the world. Upon her return to the

convent, the Foe struck her with evil thoughts of the world and of the worldly things that she had seen and heard in the world. With these thoughts he poured heavy adversity and temptation of the flesh into her. Those, she often thought to herself, she could not possibly have endured were it not for God holding her with the hand of his grace and mercy. Our dear Lord charged her with this hard and long adversity not without reason, but because he wanted to test and prove her as he had done with Saint Tobias, to whom the angel said, "Since you are so well pleasing to God, it is necessary to confirm you through adversity and hardship."[1] It is also written in the Book of Wisdom, "The Lord has tested his chosen as the gold in the furnace's fire."[2] Our Lord also charged her with this great adversity for a second reason: that her struggle would serve as an example to all those who suffer temptation and adversity.

From a young age onward, this holy virgin had received God's mercy in a tender fashion in many more sweet moments than are written about here. How often do you think she considered her virginal heart to have melted in great fear of the divine wrath? Oh, what lovely tears flowed from her eyes, because this adversity lasted for a whole year during which—as far as human strength allows—she always had to combat and resist unchastity in order to keep her heart and body pure. That is why she drove all sins and causes of sin from her, all places and people and all things that could have led to temptation. Aiming to cast away the lust of the flesh, she kept herself in a state of serious asceticism and at daytime succeeded in withstanding the Enemy who attacked her perseveringly. But at nighttime, as soon as she was supposed to go to sleep, he brought evil dreams, evil lust, and temptation to her in her sleep. In order to powerfully resist and overcome him again, whenever she woke up at night she silently got up from bed, walked over to a secret place, undressed herself, and gave herself three heavy lashes with a besom.[3] The first lash she took for all sinners, the second for all the souls in purgatory, and the third for all pious people so that God would confirm them in their righteous chastity. She did this every night for a whole year, never neglecting it for being cold or ill. All this is very minor compared to what will follow.

Although it is somewhat embarrassing to write about how she overcame her enemy and how she kept the treasure of her chastity unstained, it is still a sign of her great love. That is why I cannot possibly ignore it and I have to write something about it. When she realized that even with ardent lashes and an ascetic lifestyle she was not able to control the fire of her flesh, which the ugly Foe wanted to kindle in her day and night, she thought that she might be able to extinguish the mental fire of her flesh with material fire, since the body fears and dreads fire more than anything else. Later she not only placed her body into fire in order to stop the fire of temptation, as we read about many others who sat naked on glowing coals,[4] but she did something even greater. That a human should put their body into fire is a thing terrifying to nature; but it was even more terrifying that she put fire into her body. She did so with a great inward desire to overcome the evil spirits and their attacks of the flesh.

The next time she took a burning woodblock and rammed it into her body, while it was still glowing. Thus she extinguished the fire of her temptation with the great pain caused by material fire. I praise much more the reason and the intention behind her deed than I praise the deed itself, because it was an irrational mortification. "But for those who love God from all their heart, all things will turn to the best by God,"[5] says Saint Paul, because love covers a multitude of sins.

The discomforts of pain put an end to the temptations for a long while, until the next time, when our dear Lord wanted to test her harder by charging her very heavily with the same temptation of the flesh. Then the virgin pondered how to renew the pangs of pain in order to make her flesh ignore the lust with which the devil tempted and attacked her. This motivated her to do a horrifyingly brutal thing: she took chalk and vinegar and mixed both into a dough, which she pushed into her body as deeply as she could. Who is able to tell what great pain she suffered? As a consequence her body swelled from the feet up to the hips so much that she could not let water. This state lasted for eight full days. Afterward for three days and three nights blood came from the place where water should come from.[6] In this way she achieved such great pain that her temptation was terminated for a long time.

Another time a man came to visit whom she heard speaking to a woman about things of the flesh and the world. As she listened lustfully, forgetting to restrain her thoughts and allowing temptation, there came the Tempter, who attacked her again with the temptation of the flesh. She then repeated what she had done before, but this time using chalk and urine. Still very infirm from the first two torments she had suffered—fire and chalk—she ended up in such a state of illness from this third torment that her entire body swelled as if she were dropsical. Everyone who saw her then thought she would die.

Then she was greatly distressed and anxious that against God's will she had trespassed too greatly against prudence. So with crying eyes and with a devout heart she said to our dear Lord, "Oh loyal Lord and Father mine, are you not the sole one whom I love with all my understanding and into whom I have put all my comfort and trust? Now I beg you by the love that has bound you to the cross: if it is your will, deliver me from these bonds of body and soul." In the ensuing night, as she was lying in such great pain that her natural strength could have failed at any moment from great discomfort and grief, she said, "God never abandons those who set their hope on him." About these people the prophet says, "The Lord has heard the poor people's yearnings,[7] his eyes look to the poor. The generous comforter of all troubled hearts has looked upon his poor maiden,[8] who directed her sighs to him, and thus he comforted her in her sorrow."

At one time our Lord Jesus Christ appeared to her. She saw him with corporeal eyes and spiritual eyes as a great and mighty Lord with five wounds, each as wide as a man's hand would span. And our Lord said to her, "Look into my wounds. Are they not wide enough to conceal your discomfort in me? Here you will find medicine against all adversity." This vision so startled her that she was enraptured beyond her understanding. In this rapture God gave her the assurance that henceforth she should never again be touched by temptation of flesh; this she told me herself. And as she was praising God the Lord with all her heart, our dear Lord said to her soul (although she was not learned, she understood Latin very well in her soul), "Whenever you wish to pray, go to your chamber and secretly pray to your Father, keeping the door locked. And your Father shall hear you and reward you." There she was taught in her understanding to turn at all times to prayer, to speak only with God, and to avoid all idle speech.

11

Contra accidiam[1]

In the next year, that is the third year, great sloth came over her body; and in all her pious activities melancholia and sorrow attacked her. She withstood these with the means necessary to do so: severe mortification of body and flesh. She also worked with her hands in those days. When this blessed virgin saw that her limbs and her body were lazy and recalcitrant to serve God, she went out each morning to sit in the snow, covering her legs with snow up to the hips. So she sat until her body was as cold as the snow. Then she took a firm whip, and beat her body and her cold legs until the flesh was completely frozen from the beating. In addition she persistently practiced whatever hurt her body. No matter how cold the night, while the other nuns sat by the fire after matins, she did not want to give her body the comfort of warming it. All this she did. She deprived the body of whatever would comfort it, even of natural necessities. With such asceticism she drove all sloth away and made her body truly obedient to the spirit.

12

Contra iram[1]

In the following year she fought against anger and impatience for the duration of the entire year. Since impatience is always born of two things, she was very alert to her own comportment. She behaved like a wise combatant in the spiritual struggle because the human who wants to become spiritual is obliged to suffer gladly harsh words, hard work, and lack of necessities. The first thing that causes impatience is stubbornness of mind. The other reason for impatience is that the body is deprived of what it would like to have; for example, gentle words, friendship from people, respect, trust, security, one's own will, comfort, and anything that pleases the body. In order to also overcome impatience, she deprived the body of whatever it longed for, and whatever it detested she forced upon it. To make the body receive it patiently, she often forced upon it more than it could handle.

Sometimes she put nettles into her bed so that her whole body would be covered in blisters. Then in the mornings, when she was supposed to run to matins, she could not put on her shoes because of the blisters, and she had to celebrate mass standing barefoot on the cold stone floor. Sometimes she would fall ill because of the cold floor, and she would faint in the choir stalls as a consequence of the combination of severe afflictions: staying up all night in addition to being cold because of the stone floor, chastising her body, and overworking herself with hard labor.

She also did what required perfect continence: resisting all anger, she forced herself not to reply with an angry word, no matter how angrily someone had talked to her. Not wanting to respond impatiently and angrily with words, she would sometimes bite into her tongue so strongly that blood would shoot out of it.[2] Once, for example, she was vehemently and impatiently attacked by a woman in the convent, and, since she would have never wanted to answer this woman with any impatient word, she pressed everything into herself: it went deep into her heart until blood came out of her mouth and nose. Still, she managed not to reply to that same woman with impatient words or speech. Consider how strongly she withstood the vice of wrath.

13

Contra superbiam[1]

The fifth mortal sin is pride. With this sin she also fought for a whole year, both in spiritual and actual ways. She had overcome all pride in such a way that whatever she was not able to perform in deed she performed with desire. She adorned her body and her head as much as she could according to the customs. She withstood pride with righteous humility.

Yet one time during vespers—she had adorned her head splendidly out of pride—she looked at the cross and thought of how the lovely head of Jesus Christ was crowned and pierced with thorns. And this went so much into her heart that she threw away her head covering: instead, like a kitchen maid, she took a tea towel and wrapped it around her head. Thus she walked into the choir publicly.[2] In this manner all her pride was turned into righteous humility.

She was furthermore so keen to practice righteous humility that she often tore the washbowl out of other women's hands to do the washing up for them. In order to perfectly humble herself she submitted herself to serving the sick and taking special care of the most humiliating, ignominious, and disdained tasks. And all this she did willingly, cheerfully, and eagerly in the conviction that she did it for God himself. In this way she overcame pride with righteous humility.

14

Contra gulam[1]

She fought the sixth vice again for a whole year. It is called gula, which means dissatisfaction or the flesh's desire for food and drink beyond what nature requires. She withstood this vice with the most severe abstinence; she did not simply cut down her food and drink to what was necessary: she did not grant her body even half of what was necessary. Whenever she felt the urge to eat—even what she certainly had need of—she rather put the food aside and gave it to someone else. In short: whenever she would have loved to eat—and surely would have needed to— she stopped herself and sat there without eating. What else shall I say? She spurned herself to the point where she sometimes fainted over the table from physical weakness. In this way she fully overcame gluttony.

15

Contra odium[1]

One year she was also challenged by the seventh mortal sin, that is hatred, which often attacked her with disfavor and thoughts of vengeance against those who upset her. The vice of hatred gives birth to envy. She withstood envy very strongly and very wisely, because the Holy Spirit worked wondrous things through her in what could almost count as miracles. In order to wholly overcome this vice, she followed the counsel of our Lord Jesus Christ which we can read in the Gospel.[2] So she forced herself to serve those best who burdened and bothered her most, and who showed her the least mercy. She fulfilled their wishes, and was as kind and decent with them as she was able to be. Thus she resiliently overcame this vice with the virtue that is its counterpart, that is love of God for one's own sake and love of one's neighbor for the sake of God. Later you shall find out and hear much about how great both of these kinds of love were.

Do not be astonished that such a sensitive virgin would be so gravely led into temptation; this virgin was proven as gold is in the fire and she overcame temptation in a knightly fashion. As a child she drank the milk of the consoling and pleasant contemplation of the childhood of our Lord Jesus Christ. But in her blooming youth she was nurtured with moldy bread[3] so that she would be strengthened and prepared for higher things and perfect paths.[4]

Oh blessed virgin Christina, remember the toil with which you walked on the bitter path of this exile, and remember the merciful help of God, who has led you onto the path of justice, where henceforth you need not fear any evil; instead you now rest in the parting of your bridegroom. Therefore, oh our blessed mother, pray for all of us—because your voice is sweet to the Lord's ears—that we may safely be delivered from the sorrows of this life and enter the heavenly paradise.

16

Once this most holy virgin had overcome all vices and had been thus prepared by God the Lord for himself, he began to draw her from her exercises to higher things. Accordingly, for three years she unwaveringly practiced the contemplation of the suffering and death of our Lord. In a righteous understanding, she pondered the groundless love which had forced into martyrdom and death the dear Son of God, who is a king above all kings and above all angels, and a Lord of all Lords in heaven and on earth.[1] You, Lord, were willing to suffer hunger, thirst, and deprivation with and for us for more than thirty-three years.[2]

In ceaseless contemplation she visualized with her soul's eyes the Lord's destitution, his humiliation, his torment, and his agony, as well as his bitter Passion and his death which he so pitifully suffered on the cross. This contemplation reached so deep into her heart that she often fainted and collapsed from both the bitterness of compassion and the sweetness she received from the righteous knowledge of that loyal love which had forced him to a pitiful death on our behalf.[3] This great love broke her heart, but during her meditation such great sweetness would be bestowed upon her heart that whenever she heard the name of the tender Lord Jesus being called, her mouth was filled with sweetness because of the name of him, who had suffered death so faithfully for us.

17

In her third year of these sorts of meditative exercises she once asked to be taken to the Chapel of Saint Nicholas,[1] not long before she was going to go to bed, in order to hear mass there. This was during Lent. As she was left to sit alone in the chapel she directed her thoughts to the Passion of our Lord as was her habit. She started at the beginning of his hardship and laid everything into her heart with bitterness. So when she reached the Mount of Olives in her contemplation—reflecting on how the lovely Son of God, who is a well of all joy, had sweated blood because of deep agony and fear before his death[2]—her heart was filled with such pain that she was unable to proceed with her contemplation. For it seemed to her—as she told me herself—that had she continued the contemplation, her heart would certainly have burst within her body from the immense pain.

That her heart was inwardly and painfully wounded by the

compassion for the suffering and death of her very dearest Lord, our Lord revealed outwardly, representing it with a visible sign. At one time, when she rested her head in her left hand from severe frailty, a drop of her heart's blood fell out of her left eye and onto the finger on which one puts a ring. The ring is worn on this finger because of a vein that stretches from the heart into that finger. In this way our Lord wanted to signify that this was a drop of love which had fallen from her heart out of the eye that is close to the heart and onto that finger into which the vein from the heart runs.

The pain in her heart was also revealed in other ways. Her sisters attempted to take her back to bed, but as soon as they ever so slightly touched her left arm—the one close to the wounded heart—blood from her heart shot out of her mouth and nose; because of this great ailment she could not be moved any further and had to stay seated in the cloister for a while. Then three drops of her heart's blood fell from her left eye onto the heart's finger. Thus with much effort she was finally led to bed, where she lay forsaken by external strength, entirely forsaken.

Oh, how well was she able to speak as the bride does in the Canticum Canticorum,[3] "Tell my chosen love that I have become ill of love."[4] Oh you chosen bride of Christ, who has wounded your heart with the rays of love but the most beautiful of all human children, whose arrows are ever so sharp? Through the blissful contemplation of his love and bitter Passion, your heart was pierced with the healing rays of compassion. Obtain the mercy of devotion for us, poor children, through the contemplation of Christ's Passion, oh sweet virgin Christina!

18

———

After Love had been tormenting the blessed virgin Christina, she was led to bed, and she remained lying there as if in rapture.[1] Oh, how wonderfully God dwells in his saints, working wonders through them! Yet he who had inflicted the wound also knew well how to heal it. During the rapture her soul was carried away into a clear light, in which she saw spiritually—with the eyes of the soul—a wonderfully beautiful rose as wide as the entire earth. In the rose she saw the whole world, and all those who were in the world, and all ways of life, and all those who belonged to a religious order. And she grew very sad over all those who lived in deadly sin, as she saw both those who were in an order and those who were outside an order. Those who were in deadly sin crawled over the earth like dirty vermin. In the same light she recognized—feeling it inwardly in her soul—everything that God had ever offered to humans on earth. And as she understood in the light that his Passion, his blood, and his bitter death would be wasted on so many people, whom she saw crawling over the earth like vermin in deadly sin, she lost consciousness for four weeks due to her deep lament and heartache.

During these four weeks she lay unaware of what was happening externally. Yet whatever she saw inwardly in the spirit she often described outwardly with her mouth without being aware of it herself. Those who were near her heard it. In the same sadness and in the light our Lord said to her soul, "My soul, you shall not have sorrow nor sadness over those who have spurned me with their sins. Instead you shall rejoice that my Father has provided for all those who belong to him from the beginning on in his godhead."

She remained thus severely afflicted for four weeks and had

to be watched at night. During the four weeks our Lord gave her great gifts: with every gift the disease of her outer body changed, so that the nuns believed that she had recovered from the previous disease, but afterward she was so ill that all of them despaired of her health. These words the Lord said to her soul: "Oh my soul, I have raised you to knighthood. The angelic host moves to and fro according to my will. Oh my chosen bride, you equal the angels in virtue. You have within yourself continence,[2] obedience, ardent love; and the rank of humility you have within yourself as angels do."

19

On Holy Friday during the same Lententide she lay from before midnight until noon meditating on the suffering and death of our Lord. In this meditation she was enraptured, and in her spirit she saw all the suffering of our Lord and all the places where he suffered the Passion. All this she saw properly with the eyes of the soul, and she remained in this contemplation until the hour of none.[1] As the time approached when our Lord died on the cross after he had commended his soul to the heavenly Father, this holy virgin saw a white dove, which flew onto her head. At this, it seemed to her that her entire body cracked open for the dove to go through all her limbs, filling her with ineffable sweetness so that her pain was turned into sweetness and spiritual joy.

20

When matins was sung on the following Easter Day,[1] she lay in divine contemplation of our Lord's resurrection; and she desired from God that she would resurrect with him from her malady and from all illness of body and soul. Then our Lord appeared to her in a white gown, and embraced her kindly, and kissed her very lovingly, and said to her, "I am the life of your soul. Your salvation has embraced you." After he had spoken these words to her he left her, and she followed him but she was not able to catch up. So he walked ahead of her through the cloister and into the chapterhouse until he reached a grave. At once, in the spirit, she recognized who was lying buried in the grave. Our Lord kneeled down on the gravestone and made the sign of the cross over the grave. She finally caught up with him at the grave, and as she sought to embrace him he disappeared from her eyes. Then she heard, spiritually only, a great host of angels singing very sweetly in the air, "The Lord has risen from his grave," and many other very beautiful words. And the angels led many souls with great joy into the heavens, in particular the soul from the grave on which our Lord had knelt and over which he had made the sign of the cross. She saw the name of the same person written in golden letters.

On the same day during mass, she strongly desired the holy sacrament of her beloved bridegroom. When after mass the priest brought her our Lord, it seemed to her that the entire infirmary was full of divine light and sweet fragrance. When she had received our Lord with great love and in ineffable love and desire, her heart was filled with sweetness as if all of her limbs were full of sweetness. In this delight and sweetness she heard the angels singing in the air very joyfully the entire "Gloria in excelsis." In this light of rapture our Lord made the blessed virgin Christina understand that this was the 1,288th year since his birth.[2]

21

On the eve of Pentecost[1] she sat alone in vigil in her choir stall all night until matins in a consuming and ardent desire for God to send her the light and fire of the Holy Spirit, that her soul might be illuminated in the knowledge and inflamed in the love as the holy apostles were kindled. In this desire, her soul melted in her body with many tears before midnight. Then she saw with the eyes of her soul a magnificent and delightful eagle hovering above her. His eyes burned like a torch, radiating a bright light and leaving it behind wherever he flew. There she understood in a divine manner that the eagle was her very dearest Lord. And she yearned with loving desire that he would turn his wings to her and give himself generously into her soul, which—absorbed in his love—longed for him. At this, the very dearest swung his wings in her direction, once, twice—and just as often he turned away from her again. This amplified everything in her even more, both love and desire. Finally, while her soul toiled in a wondrous desire, the King of Heaven descended into her soul. She was filled with wondrous joy and showered with divine delight. Then the Lord embraced her soul with his divine arms, and he also commanded her to embrace him with her bodily arms, and he pressed her against his heart.

But then morning dawned, and as she was supposed to go and receive him who loved her, it seemed to her that she was walking in delight, her feet not touching the ground, because love was carrying her. Then she saw that the church was full of divine grace. With the sacrament, handed to her by the priest, she then received her most beloved Lord, and her soul was filled with such special joy and grace that she melted in sweet delight like honey, and she once more sank into a blissful light. There she saw in the spirit that the heavens were open and that a great light was in them. A light, shining and burning, came down from heaven. The light was like the entire earth, and in it she saw a living heart, which was opening and closing itself. Whenever it opened itself, a wonderful light poured out, illuminating heaven and earth and all therein, and filling everything with indescribable joy. "O sapientia Jesu Christi"[2] was written on the heart and more, but she could not recall the rest. Then she desired that the light, together with the heart, would enter her soul, and exactly this happened. She embraced the light,[3] and then she became hot from the ardent love, and she was wholly illuminated by the divine light.

Because of the great sweetness and wondrous knowledge she asked, "Oh wonderful God, what are you?" Immediately she received a response from the divine heart: "I am a burning fire, a bright light. I am a voice, a will. I am all the abundant sweetness you need, and everything that all desiring hearts and all saints need."[4] This drew her into a divine contemplation, and because of this sweet contemplation she became unconscious. She was so hot from love and so inwardly burning from the soul's heat that her body, too, caught a great outward heat. It was so hot that this truly burning great heat could not be extinguished with cold water, which those who were with her often tried for a long time. The virtue of love wrestled with her with such vehemence that her beloved was forced into her soul and the body risked being torn apart from the inside. Mighty Love took the lead and Christina had to suffer ailments according to God's will, and she did so with pleasure.[5] This was a blessed Pentecost for her.

22

On the feast when Holy Christendom celebrates the mass of Corpus Christi[1] she again desired to receive her dear Lord with great affection.[2] While the priest was carrying the holy sacrament she saw inwardly, through the walls of the building, that the priest was bringing our Lord as a bright light.[3] In this light it seemed to her that she received communion from God's hands, although she actually received communion from the priest's hands. To her our Lord was as sweet as honey in her mouth, and this sweetness flowed into her heart and into her soul.

Then he who loved her spoke to her soul, "Love, love me. I come swiftly and rejoice in you. Love, love me. I come swiftly and comfort you. Love, love me. I come swiftly and summon you." This sweet vision and enjoyment of the soul[4] was at that time bound to end. It usually happened to her as she received our Lord—when he would become so sweet in her mouth that the sweetness went into her soul and heart, and flowed through all her limbs—and would last until our Lord transformed her into something better and higher.[5]

Now, in one such vision concurrent with receiving the communion, she spiritually saw a tree growing out of her heart. Its roots were green, signifying that the heart shall be divinely green with virtues and good deeds and holy thoughts and with sweet desire. The trunk was pure and clear; this signifies the pure clarity of our heart.[6] The tree was well adorned and beautiful and in full blossom on top. Each blossom had a distinct color; this signifies that in the heavenly kingdom God clothes and adorns the soul with manifold virtues. On each blossom there sat a little bird, and above them on the highest blossom sat a large and beautiful bird, like an eagle.[7] Its eyes were like a bright light, and with a sweet voice it sang to the other birds the following words: "Ego sum panis vivus," etc. At this all the other birds followed him in song with a beautiful melody: "Tu es panis vivus, in quo omnes vivimus in eternum."[8] Then the top bird, our Lord Jesus Christ, opened up like a light, and the small birds flocked around him, and he enclosed all of them in himself. Then the heavens opened up and within him gathered them all in, with great joy. "Then my spirit remained in the light for three days and three nights. God granted me much to see and much to know in heaven and on earth, which I cannot all tell."[9]

23

On the feast day of Saint John the Baptist[1] this holy virgin was in fervent devotion, as was her habit. As was her habit, she was in fervent devotion and desire. So she was lifted up in the spirit into a magnificent light, where the dear bridegroom played with his bride, and he said to her, "Oh very dearest soul of mine, demand of me whatever you wish. You, chosen soul of mine, whom I have chosen for myself, demand of me whatever you wish. I am the divine love, and the son of life has clothed you with eternal light. I have granted you eternal life and all that is good. Wisdom is your life in the eternal godhead."

The light in this rapture lasted for six weeks. During these six weeks she was deprived of her external hearing because of the power of the internal light. In the light she frequently saw that much fraud and betrayal was happening in Rome, and she saw other things that were taking place in the curia.[2] She was able to look into the heart of anyone who came before her during this period. She saw what was hidden in their heart and recognized it. Anything that was spoken in the convent, she could hear; also where it was spoken, she could hear inwardly in the intellect of the soul.[3] During this period she could not eat anything but sweet food due to her heart being in a unique sweetness. So when she sometimes desired honey or figs, she saw spiritually where the nuns kept them in their chests and other places. Seeing this, she then demanded it of them.

In the same light she saw that a great battle would take place near Cologne and that many people would be killed then. She reported this to those who were near her. When the day and the hour of the battle finally arrived, she saw spiritually that eleven thousand people were killed and that all their souls went to hell. She likewise saw that her biological brother carried the bishop's banner and that all those belonging to his family would be captured but not killed.[4] All this she saw spiritually and reported to those who were near her. They later found out that everything had happened on the day and on the hour she had foretold.

During the same six weeks our Lord said to her, "Three sisters are going to die one after the other: before the next one dies, the previous one will be released from purgatory." At this she raised her voice with joy, saying, "We shall love, we shall praise, we shall behold!" From the latter can be inferred that she had prayed to the Lord for these biological sisters, the way she had often prayed for the living and the dead. Those living and dead amounted to an uncountable number, as you shall hear later.

24

As this holy virgin was thus spiritually enraptured, she spoke the following words: "Love is kindled by fire, it is lit by light. Remember the beloved:[1] the high, sweet, and pure godhead that is joined to your soul." In the same light she said to our dear Lord, "Oh my gentle love, the way I have begged you before for the living and the dead, so I beg you now that you may not deny my prayer." Our dear Lord replied to her, "Oh my very dearest, I have assured you an eternal life with a secure guarantee."

At the same time, while she was unconscious and in divine contemplation wholly united with him, her external senses were sleeping. The chosen one sang a lovely song to her, but he did not sing with the kind of voice that can be heard aloud. However, she sang with a voice that everyone near her heard, and they later told her about it. Once she came back to her senses she could not remember what had happened and why she knew the words and the tune that the Lord had sung to her soul, which was as follows: "The remembrance of Jesus is sweet and the heart's sweet joy. Hail, crown of thorns, blessed be the person whose royal head you have pierced! Oh crown of thorns, grant me the kingdom and the empire through Christ's prayer! Oh jewel of Christendom, oh honorable thorn, a crown of the king of honor, oh remedy to the world, sweetness and balm to our distress, deliver from evil all those who praise you today!"[2]

25

In the same light this holy virgin had a spiritual vision: she saw above herself, up in the air, that a man was murdering his wife with a shovel by beating her on the ground until she was dead. Seeing this in the spirit, she screamed and cried and said, "Woe, the murderer must be called out!" The nuns who were with her heard her shouting. She also saw that the same woman was not only dead of body but also dead of soul, since she had died with the intention of avenging herself by murdering her husband. She furthermore perceived spiritually that the man was forever lost and that he was going to die a terrible death.[1] Soon afterward he died accordingly: it did not take long until he was drowned in the Rhine for another malicious act. However, at the time when he had killed his wife, she saw in the spirit that he transported the corpse to the convent in order to get his wife buried therein. She reported this to all the nuns who were with her, so they found out about it. Then, as soon as the magistra[2] and the others heard about it, they rushed to the windows, where they saw that someone was coming from the direction of a village; he was carrying a dead woman and asked them to bury her in the convent. This is how she made it known that this man had killed his wife, and as a consequence he was forced to flee the country.

26

In the same light she saw spiritually that a knight had killed the brother of her sister-in-law in a city called Lahnstein.[1] With this she also saw that his soul was forever lost, which made her cry sorrowfully. So it was with great sadness that she reported to the nuns who were present that his soul was lost. She named the knight and the city where this happened, which surprised the nuns very much since it occurred far away in a different country. For this reason they inquired about it and found out that what she had seen and heard and consequently told them had indeed happened there on that very day.

She equally saw in the same light a second thing: two of her brother's children, a boy and a girl, would die within a fortnight and ascend to heaven.[2] As was her habit, she told this too to the nuns who were near her. Truly everything she saw during these six weeks she later did not recall at all. Yet whatever she saw inwardly in the spirit, her bodily mouth simultaneously uttered outwardly, which she was not aware of. After she had told the nuns about the two children they found out that both of them had died at the time she had foretold.

27

This holy virgin was also especially devoted to the royal Virgin Mary, the Mother of God. In the same way the Mother of God was especially inclined to favor her for the sake of her Son's love. Once, as the verse "Audi nos" of the sequence "Ave praeclara" was sung in the convent, she saw the Mother of God on her knees praying for the convent.[1]

At another time, as the evening bell was rung to sing the "Ave Maria," she hurried so much to fall down to the ground that she wounded her knee severely.[2] The very sweetest Virgin and mildest Mother Mary noticed this, and she comforted her most loyal servant, appearing to her in her sleep carrying in her tender hands a vessel filled with exquisite balms. So she healed her servant, and she commanded her to kneel down more gently thenceforth.

28

On one occasion the Mother of God admonished her because of the exaggerated penitential practices to which she submitted herself, as you have already heard. At that time she was in the

Chapel of Saint Nicholas praying with the full devotion of her heart in front of the sculpture of Our Dear Lady.[1] The sculpture on the altar stretched out her virginal hand and slapped her in the face, thus punishing her in a motherly way. Then she said to her, "Be content with what is common." Suddenly she became self-aware. So she stood up and turned to the crucifix next to the altar, prostrating herself in front of it; and with deep and heart-felt remorse she begged for mercy in the Son's eyes, and she also begged to be spared from the Mother's anger, and she desired mercy from the Lord.

29

After six weeks, during which this blessed virgin was enraptured in a divine light where she saw and heard plenty which is not written here, the feast of Assumptio beatae et gloriosae virginis Mariae arrived.[1] Among the many acts of mercy and sweetness that she received, our Lord particularly brought to her and in-structed her in the seven precepts, which are proper for those who want to love and please God.[2] The first is that one shall withdraw from worldly things, because whoever lends his heart to ephemeral things deprives his heart of mercy. The second is that one shall direct the thoughts of one's heart to God at all times, which makes the heart spiritual. The third, that one shall turn and devote oneself to the contemplation of God: this illu-minates the soul. The fourth, that one shall never forsake his friends: this is true love. The fifth, that one shall set up one's heart with desire for one's beloved at all times: this brings divine espousal. The sixth, that one shall always hold God before one's eyes, that you do anything he likes and avoid anything he dislikes and patiently suffer anything he charges you with. The seventh, that you never—because of anyone's love or hatred—forget what you have to do with God.

30

On the feast of the Nativity of the Blessed Virgin Mary this blessed virgin received our Lord with great love and inward desire.[1] At this a bright light embraced her soul inwardly, and the highest sweetness poured over her heart and all her limbs. In this light she saw spiritually a tree growing out of her soul like a palm tree. On top the tree was very wide and large, and on the bottom it was thin and small. In this light the Lord made her understand about this tree and its significance as is written in Canticum canticorum:[2] "I shall climb up into the palm tree and I shall embrace its fruit."[3]

Note that on the bottom the tree is thin and it stings, but on top it is wide with leaves and it bears noble fruit. In the same way, her life in this age has been small because of humble self-knowledge; she was often stung by bitter sorrow through abstinence from food and drink, through ailments, and through rough clothes and beds, as you have heard before. But above she was all-encompassing[4] in divine love toward her enemies and friends, noble in the sweet fruits of virtue. You still are to hear great miracles after this; about how her taste delighted God in heaven, how it likewise delighted the angels and all the saints, the sinners on earth and the dear souls in purgatory. In that light the Lord said to her soul: "I have erected your life with complete humility. I have adorned you with complete purity. I have made you rich with patience, and I have reinforced you in love,[5] and I have lifted you up from the lowest to the highest."

31

On Saint Michael's Day[1]

This holy virgin had such a great ardent love for her very dearest Lord and for receiving him in the holy sacrament that when the priest brought him she recognized inwardly that the noble body of God, luminously radiant, approached her quickly. In this divine light she saw the priest approaching her carrying our dear Lord, even before she saw him with her bodily eyes. At once she saw that there were four majestic candle bearers, two walking in front and two behind. With a celestial voice they sang all of the "Te sanctum dominum in excelcis," including the "Gloria patri." Then, as soon as the priest opened the vessel, she sensed the very sweetest taste and scent, which strengthened and vivified her heart and body, and all her limbs, which had been ailing because of her great desire. As the priest offered her the holy body she saw the most beautiful child alive: white and red, it was perfectly beautiful. Around its head was written "I am the beginning and the end."[2]

And she told me: "At the time when I received my very dearest love, my soul melted from the sweetest infirmity and it was lowered into an abyss of delightful love. Then the beloved said to my soul, 'You are my chosen bride, my dove, my queen. I will make you noble with my wisdom.'

"At this my soul was divinely taken up into a large and magnificent royal house filled with joy and bliss. Therein gathered a crowd of all the chosen ones who have ever lived on earth. I recognized many of them, despite never having known or seen them before. In the center of the house grew a tree rising up to the sky. Half of the tree bore roses and the other half lilies, because the tree's fruit nurtured all the chosen ones and God with them. The tree trunk was split in the middle, and a celestial light shone out of it. In this light God's voice spoke: 'I am the light of the world.[3] All of you are truly blessed. You are all co-heirs of my Father. You blossom before me like lilies.' Then the beloved said to me, 'O my soul, do you see light in light? I entrust to you the living and the dead. I will open my wounds to you.'

"After this my indulged soul laid down on the one who loved it.[4] It was unified with him in a sweet rest, in a loving sleep."

32

On the feast day of the Holy Eleven Thousand Virgins,[1] as the blessed virgin was about to receive the holy sacrament, her soul burned with great love. When the priest brought the holy sacrament she saw a fiery light, and in this light she saw her very dearest Lord approaching. Before him walked a great host of angels, like an army of knights before a king, and they all sang with a sweet noise. The infirmary was filled with an oversweet smell. At that time her heart would have burst in her body if she had been kept away from her soul's beloved for any longer. As the priest opened the vessel—she was yearning impatiently for her chosen one—she saw a little lamb sleeping in the vessel. It had a wreath around its head on which was written with golden letters: "Agnus dei qui tollit peccata mundi."

"Suddenly the lamb woke up and swiftly leapt into the priest's hands, and it reached toward me as it desired me." When she had received the lovely lamb of God, her soul was filled with oversweet joy. Her soul was spiritually led to a royal palace which was as wide as the whole earth. In its center stood God's mighty throne. There were chairs everywhere in the palace. The chairs were wrought with lilies, and everything was filled with the sweetest scent. There she saw her very dearest Lord in the shape of a lamb, and he said to her, "I am the true living lamb that creates and orders all things in you." The Father's voice also spoke to her: "My dear Son shall be with you until the end of the world."

On the lamb's back was a flag which had three points reaching into different directions. One point covered the entire palace; this was Christendom, which he preserves and protects with his patient mercy. Another point went into purgatory, in order to comfort the souls and ease their pain. The third point covered the heavens, signifying all those whom he wants to save. He illuminates them and fills them with his divine grace. Yet the queen, Our Lady, receives the greatest infusion of divine light and bliss, as she is the first to receive it before all other saints.

Then the flag was transformed into a mirror, in which Christina saw Our Lady with all holy virgins. She recognized them by name, and saw how each of them was rewarded and honored by God. Of the eleven thousand she recognized in particular the names and families of those whose heads are kept in our chapel.[2] The names are still recorded in the convent scrolls; they are the following: Ceomate virgo, Petrisse virgo, Elyzabet virgo, Benedicta virgo, Juliana virgo, Anne virgo, Cunigondis virgo, Gertrudis virgo, Cristine virgo, Cristine virgo, Elyzabet filiae cesaris.

The divine lamb sang a very sweet melody and the virgins repeated all of it with cheerful voices and heartfelt joy; they joined with him and he with them without a single difference. Hey, what a good gathering! Hey, what a good dance! Hey, what a good song! Hey, what a lovely pastime![3] This was the round dance that he taught them: "Holy, holy are you in my godhead, perfect in my eternal love."[4] Afterward he said to them: "I am the path of perfection which brings high and great love. I am the pure truth which was prepared for you from the beginning on and in the beginning." Then her soul reclined onto her beloved's bosom into a sweet peace and a loving embrace.

33

On the feast day of All Saints[1] this holy virgin longed with great desire to hear the mass of the day. Great desire was excited within her: at once she heard the angelic host singing sweetly in the air the entire "Te deum laudamus." This enraptured her even more. On this day she needed help to get to the place of worship. As they were approaching the house of the Lord, she saw that the church[2] and all its surroundings were filled with celestial scent and light.

As mass began in the choir, she saw in the air a prepared magnificent altar. The altar was adorned with lilies on top, with roses at the front, and with violets on both sides. There, our Lord was priest, Saint Gabriel was deacon, and Saint Michael was subdeacon. Our Lord's chasuble was as translucent as a clear stone so that one could look through him and see from behind him what was happening in front of him. Then the Lord started singing mass with the sweetest voice, and the full celestial choir sang; with ineffable joy they sang the entire mass.

Suddenly, when the moment came that he should elevate the holy sacrament, a fiery light appeared. It radiated its gleam to all the saints in heaven and on earth, and to holy Christendom; it also reached into purgatory, a comfort and mercy to all the souls. After he had broken the host into three parts, she saw, on the part that was put into the chalice, the crucified Jesus with bleeding wounds hanging on a cross. She also saw the same on the two other parts. The chalice was as deep as if it were bottomless, and the holy blood flowed through hidden veins.[3]

Then the community went up and our Lord gave them communion. However, she saw that our Lord dwelled with some and passed others by. As he said, "Ite missa est," and gave his blessing, all those worthy of it were revealed to her. Those who were worthy received white wreaths on their heads. In the meantime—while the nuns went up to our Lord, who gave them communion—the priest had finished reading the mass in the choir.

Then she saw the most beautiful little lamb playing merrily on the altar. On his back was a red cross. At once the little lamb sprang swiftly to her and cavorted around her cheerfully, and this filled her soul with glee. Then the priest gave her the one who loved her, whom she received with a great joy full of overflowing sweetness. The true lamb mercifully clasped her soul inwardly, saying to her in this loving embrace, "Oh you most lovely, rejoice, rejoice. You have your soul's heavenly savior in you; who is a king of all kings, God, Son of God; who with his mercy can satisfy your hunger and can extinguish your thirst with his sweetness."

Because of this her soul was enraptured and lowered into such a great love that heaven and earth and also purgatory were simultaneously opened up to her. She recognized many people and many things in all these three places. Thus she remained in ineffable love—a delight that God had with the soul—for three days and nights, all while being unconscious and oblivious of her external senses.

34

On the following Holy Christmas in 1289, when the moment of Christ's birth had come, she was in great devotion, joyous about the feast day. Her body was overflowing with a merciful sweetness, and a celestial light appeared in her and above her. In this light the celestial queen, Mary, came forth holding her very sweetest infant Jesus in her motherly arms; and she laid the lovely child into Christina's heart. Jesus, her only love, played a dearly sweet game of love with her soul, which no tongue may speak of, nor can any hand write about.

While her soul relished her heart's love in sweet desire, the gorgeous Virgin and Mother Mary sang a lovely ditty with a sweet and cheerful voice for three consecutive hours. The infant Jesus sang with her the following: "Oh my very dearest companion, I have granted you salvation and eternal life." This vision, including the song, happened entirely in the spirit and was not perceived in external senses.

35

On Epiphany[1]

Twelve days later, on Epiphany in 1289,[2] she received the worthy holy sacrament with great love and desire. In that moment her love spoke within her, that is, not with an external voice but within her soul, telling her what his desire was. "I grant you my three very dearest gifts: I forgive you all your sins; I draw you to me; I confirm you in myself as if it were a fact that you had never sinned. Moreover, I shall give you these in overflowing measure."[3]

The overflowing measure meant that she saw everything and that she turned all of it to the best possible outcome. As she was thus being cared for in his love, he said to her, "I love you, oh blessed soul, with all my heart. I have heard you from my high throne."

36

On the feast day of Purificatio,[1] when this devout virgin was supposed to receive her very dearest Lord, she was led into the Chapel of Saint Nicholas, where she waited for her love. Her anguish was so great that her soul, consumed in an ardent desire, longed for an end to the waiting. A light went into her soul that shone and burned both inwardly and outwardly. The priest came from the choir to bring the lovely body of God. She saw it being brought, for the light shone in her soul and through the walls. This was not a miracle. God is a burning fire. This is why she saw him before he had reached her. Once she was given the holy sacrament her soul melted from sweet love and lovely sweetness—like honey does near fire—in order to enjoy divine delight. The divine light was with her.

When the nuns—there were nearly thirty of them—went up to receive the holy sacrament, she saw in the divine light—that is, she saw not with external eyes—what happened to nine of them whose names she knew well: their hearts opened like roses that unlock in the dew and thrust out their petals against the sun, flourishing fully. And she saw that the very dearest infant Jesus lovingly took a seat in these roses; and the roses closed up. The roses signify the love of chaste hearts. This increased the love and joy in her soul with the greatest sweetness. Afterward she asked one of the nine nuns how she had felt when receiving the holy sacrament. The same nun answered her that it had been a long time since she last felt such magnanimous mercy, sweetness, and comfort from receiving the holy sacrament as she had then.

37

On the feast day of the Annunciation of Mary[1] this indulgent soul had no rest other than in the one who loved her. So she practiced loving desire, as she had done many times before when receiving the highly praised Lord. He then celebrated merry nuptials with her soul in the overflowing sweetness of his presence.

God revealed to her a royal palace, greater than the whole world and green like grass inside. It was filled with beauty and might; and complete joy resided in it; and it was entirely laid out with chairs. One jolly and graceful throne stood out, set in the center and composed of three different seats. One of the seats was made of roses, another of lilies, the third of violets. This throne with its distinctive seats stood closest to the place of the celestial queen, and it signifies the three different types of people who are closest to God, as was revealed to her: the roses mean completely loyal lovers, the lilies mean pure chaste hearts, the violets signify true humility.

She saw that the very dearest Lord was happily present in her soul. His eyes burned in his face like a torch. A rose grew out of his heart; it blossomed and extended its petals so wide and thick that it covered his entire body like a robe. The rose continued growing and miraculously sprawled out; with its petals it powerfully covered the whole palace, forming a vault above it. This signifies that the loyal love, which grows out of the divine heart, is above all honor and above all the love of angels and of people. Love forced him to become human, and he suffered death for the sake of our redemption. This love goes beyond and exceeds all other forms of love.

As she was in this sweet contemplation—she was enjoying

God with an overflowing sweetness in this palace—the dear Lord embraced her soul in a truly amicable manner, that is, with an embrace of both arms. He also poured into her his intention: that here in this life he embraces his chosen ones in his left arm with sweet grace, and after this life he embraces them in his right arm with eternal joy. Then the Lord said to her soul, "Rejoice, my soul. You have received me as certainly as my mother received me in her pure and virginal body. I would much rather dwell in you than in my heaven." After this her soul surrendered itself, entering into a sweet peace and love in God.

38
—

Of Easter

On Easter the soul of the blessed virgin was in a divine light in which she saw many wonders and found ineffably great mercy. In the same light God revealed to her ten pieces of divine wisdom.[1]

The first: that one recognizes the moment God arrives with his mercy in the soul; and this comes with a sweet and cheerful motion of the heart.

The second piece of wisdom is that one recognizes the moment God departs from the soul; this is when he takes away the mercy of sweet comfort, leaving her behind in sadness.

The third piece of wisdom lies in the ardent love and desire for God.

The fourth piece of wisdom is that one recognizes when a virtuous life falters. The virtues diminish when devotion and fiery desire begin to fade and cool down. However little you pray, fast, and keep vigil, or even if you stop doing such external exercises altogether, your virtuous life will not falter as long as you keep in you the fire and the light of love—even if all external exercise lies dead—because external exercises are worth less than internal ones, just as copper is worth less when compared to gold.

The fifth piece of wisdom: that one recognizes all sins and vices, so that one's pure conscience may prevent the concealment of anything which damages the soul.

This sixth piece of wisdom is that one recognizes what is good; that is, divine grace, all virtues, and the patient endurance of hardship in the body, in frailty, in physical needs, in humiliation, and all such things that may entail mercy and reward.

The seventh piece of wisdom: that one knows how to wisely part from evil. For it is the very best wisdom to be able to counter and overcome any temptation, in both the spirit and the flesh.

The eighth piece of wisdom is that one knows how to wisely exercise virtues and good deeds. That is why God grants mercy and spiritual gifts: that one may invest them wisely and make a profitable practice of virtues; just as a father trusts a pound or more into his son's hands, that he may wisely invest it and gain profit like a wise salesman. If he invests it well he will get more, but if he is neglectful the father will take it from him and give it to someone else, so says the Gospel.[2]

The ninth piece of wisdom is that one orients one's heart toward just things—may it be toward God and one's own fellow Christians, toward prelates, toward subjects, toward friends, toward enemies, toward oneself—so that everything may remain on a just path.

The tenth piece of wisdom: that one praises God in all things and in all creatures as a wise creator and sustainer, and that one praises him in all that he imposes on a person—whether done on earth, in heaven, or in the abyss. This praise originates in a good will that is united with God.

The gentle noble bridegroom has prepared his bride according to his pleasure. That is why she has always had a body afflicted with pain and a soul filled with all that is good. She was bedridden with a wounded body—both inwardly and outwardly it suffered great ailments—as you may hear in the following two cases: of God's imposition and of great abstinence.

39

Three nuns used to care for this bride of Christ the Lord, with great diligence and great devotion. Because they were so immensely loyal to her, she shared with them her benefits. Whenever she was comforted by and enjoying her very dearest Lord, she begged him to have mercy on them. Because of this, our Lord granted them great and special mercy, as will become apparent. He did so because a person is served best when their dear friends are treated well. We have a positive example for such treatment in our Lord Jesus Christ, when he entrusted his mother to Saint John for him to care for.[1] For that reason Jesus granted John special mercy. He let him rest on his bosom and always favored him especially, as we often read about John.[2] So it was for these holy nuns. Because they served this chosen companion of God so loyally, our Lord granted them the special mercy of salvation and blessed their bodies and souls.

Truly, whoever reads this book and considers the miracle of mercy and divine love, which God granted this chaste virgin, his chosen bride Christina, is able to confirm that he who has been chosen by God to serve blessed beings is born blessed. Thus spoke our Lord into her soul about these three nuns: "These three nuns are blessed and they carry chaste hearts in my name."

This was only the beginning of many friendly words which God often amicably uttered in her soul about these three nuns.

Oh, you will hear later of the lovely conversation God usually maintained. Below you will find many words about the great sensation of mercy and sweetness, gained through miraculous inward contemplations—words that are as inexpressibly incomprehensible to our rough minds as German is to a foreigner.[3] Here, then, are written some of the sweet words, arranged according to the feast days; they shall lead the hearts who love God to praise God for his grace and worthiness, which is understood in manifold ways.

40

On the feast day of Saint Agnes[1] the Lord said to her soul, "Oh very dearest soul of mine, I am a light of your heart. You are my beloved and I am he who rests in you. You shall remain my eternal bride, forever."

41

On the feast of Purificatio beatae Mariae virginis[1] her soul was united with God. Listen, what he said to her then: "Oh my blessed companion, I am the sweet love that lives in your soul. I am the one who illuminates it. I am its eternal light, it sees into me. Therefore you shall have joy upon joy, without end."

42

On Dominica Invocavit[1] the Lord said to her who loved him, "I am your bridegroom. I am a light of the purity of wisdom to you.

Oh my most beloved bride, set me as a seal upon your heart.[2] Embrace me like a friend with heartfelt love, and conquer me with your arms saying the following words: 'Love is as strong as death.'" Etc.

43

On Maundy Thursday[1] the Lord said to her, "I am the eternal light. I am the living sun that shines through and into your heart. I give myself to you and I join myself to your soul. You are my chosen bride and I am your beloved."

44

After Easter she heard the following words: "I am the father of the light with which your soul is eternally illuminated. God is in your soul and your soul is in God, and it remains with him at all times."

45

On the feast day of Saint John Before the Latin Gate[1] he said, "Oh, you are my chosen and I am your chosen. I give you celestial food and I give myself fully to you. Oh my chosen one, give me your flowery heart in which I will rest with your soul."

Three days later the Lord said to her, "I am the living mirror which illuminates heaven and earth and sea and everything that dwells in it. In this mirror your soul is illuminated."

46

On the feast day of our Lord's Ascension[1] our Lord said to her, "I am a light which illuminates all light, in which all things live without end, in which your soul remains forever."

47

On Pentecost[1] the Lord said to her, "I am a burning light. I illuminate all light. I am a sweet voice. I am food. I give all that is good, all that is sweet, and I fill heaven and earth with my magnitude. Rejoice, my very dearest soul. You shall be where God is, and you shall be unified with God."

48

On the feast day of Corpus Christi[1] the Lord said to her, "I am the living word and I dwell in your heart, and you are a temple of my heart. Oh my chosen soul, rejoice. I love you. Oh my soul, rejoice. You are my chosen one, you shall enter heaven and rejoice with my chosen ones."

49

On the feast of the Nativity of Saint John the Baptist[1] she was in a state of deep contemplation and sweet desire. The beloved said to her, "My very dearest soul, demand of me whatever you wish. Oh best chosen one of mine, demand of me whatever you wish. I am the divine love. The sun of life has clothed you with eternal light. You receive from me everything that is good. Wisdom is your life in the eternal godhead."

In the same light the Lord said to her soul, "Oh gentle soul of mine, you are mine and I am yours, I will be with you forever. I am the glorious God, the abundant God, the mighty God, the eternal God, the wise God." The Lord also said to her, "Now join together all of these attributes in your soul. So I am glorious in abundance and I am abundant glory, the mighty wisdom and the wise might, the blessed eternity and the eternal blessedness."

50

On the day of Saint Udalricus[1] the Lord spoke with the one who loved him, saying to her, "Oh my one and only soul, I have granted you salvation with the kiss of my mouth. Rejoice, my one and only soul. You have within you your chosen Lord Jesus Christ. You are my one and only dove. I shall celebrate nuptials with your soul."

51

On the feast day of Saint Mary Magdalene[1] the Lord said to her, "Oh my one and only soul, your life is very dear. You have full power over me. I will hear your prayer and I will accomplish your will. The souls for which you have prayed to me shall soon be redeemed." She had prayed for a thousand souls and for the soul of Hertwig.[2] For these souls she had had three hundred masses sung.

The Lord said to her soul, "Oh most blessed soul, I have welcomed you to me. So I shall love you forever. I rest in you as I rest in my merry kingdom. I will make you equal to me as much as is possible."

52

On the feast day of the Assumption of the Blessed Virgin Mary[1] this blessed virgin practiced her habitual sweet contemplation and desire before she received her very sweetest Lord. He said to her, "Oh sweetest soul of mine, rejoice. I love you. You shall embrace me with holy awe and holy love: these are the arms of your soul, with which you shall embrace me lovingly. Once you have thus embraced me, hold me as tight as you can; then I will flow over you and lower you into the angelic sweetness." Her soul replied with ineffable love: "Oh daughters of Jerusalem, tell my love that I have become ill of love."[2]

He also spoke to her on the day of the Beheading of Saint John:[3] "Here on earth I chastise my very dearest friends. I shield my dear friends from the fortunes of this world. I discipline my very dearest friends with my paternal rod."[4] Etc.

53

On the feast day of the Nativity of the Blessed Virgin Mary[1] the Lord said to her soul, "Oh very dearest soul of mine, I am a burning god. I am a powerful god. I am an illuminating god. I am an illuminator of souls. I am he who widens your heart in the love of eternal life. With my help I make your soul fertile. I have longed to see your face." Then she said to her chosen one, "My most beloved, descend into your garden."[2] The Lord replied to her in a sweet voice, "I am a flower of your heart and the peace of your soul."

54

On the feast day of Saint Michael[1] the Lord said to her, "Oh honorable soul, I love you. I will make you virtuous. I will seat you in my adorned kingdom and in the choir of angels—of archangels, cherubim and seraphim—who through my love are kindled by burning love. With them, my very dearest, you shall joyously remain forever, without end. There you shall drink my new wine streaming from the constantly flowing sweetness of my godhead and divine nature. Oh my companion, I am your heart and soul's joy, and a mirror of your eyes."

55

On the day of the Eleven Thousand Virgins[1] the Lord said to her, "Oh my chosen bride, rejoice, because your sweetest bridegroom loves you. I play in you the game of love. My joy and my delight are in you. Your soul is divinely united with me. You, my bride, recognize me in the purity of your heart, and you sweetly rest in me at all times."

56

On the feast day of All Saints[1] the very dearest one spoke in sweet conversation to his chosen one: "Oh very dearest soul, what more could you now desire?[2] You have a truly ardent lover. You live according to my will. Oh very dearest soul of mine, what more could you wish for? You have a soul filled with the divine. The thousand souls for which you had prayed to me, and also Hertwig's soul, I have this night delivered of the agonies that they suffered in purgatory, because of your love. These souls you shall joyously behold in me. Oh most blessed soul of mine, what more could you now wish for? Your body is full of your good deeds. Your lover lives in you for these thousand souls. Through your love, your eternal God has brought them to joy as free and unchained souls on the eve of All Saints."

Thus spoke this blessed virgin: "When I was in this loving light I saw magnificent love and wonderful wonders, and how very dearly and amicably the loving God welcomed the afore-mentioned souls into the celestial lodging. The celestial Father was the host; the Son was the steward; and the Holy Spirit was the cupbearer, who was giving them Cyprian wine to drink, of which it is written in the Book of Love, 'I shall give my chosen one to drink from the wine of the grapes of Cyprus.'[3] Then our Lord said to the blessed souls, 'Come, you blessed of my Father, into the kingdom, which is prepared for you from the begin-ning.'"[4]

Afterward she saw how God seated each soul according to its worthiness.[5] There she recognized that the souls became God and that they absorbed the divine love in an ineffable sweetness. Then God and the blessed souls were eternally unified into one will. These souls were immediately filled with divine sweetness, and they were so nourished with celestial bread that they for-got all their hardship. Then they melted into God with ineffable enjoyment of the sweet godhead and the dear humanity. These souls diffused into God with pure love so that all their intellect[6] was filled with joy. Whenever God pours his divine light into souls, they overflow of an ineffable oversweetness and an over-sweet delight. Then they say with great joy: "We have received our savior and our beatitude. We shall now never let go of him."

Each soul becomes drunk on love and on the joy of all the saints.[7] Therefore they will swim in great love; and they will sink into the divine mirror, in which they will see new wonders and never-ending new joys. Then, because of the mighty marvels that they will see in God, they will say the following words: "Oh almighty Lord, half of what we feel now we did not perceive when we still lived on earth. Oh Lord, blessed are those who dwell in your house. For ever and ever shall they praise you."

57

On the day of All Saints the blessed virgin was unified with her love in spiritual delight. Her prayers to her love were for the living and the dead. She heard his sweet voice saying to her spirit, "Oh most sweet-tempered soul of mine, what more could you desire? You have a heart full of holy desire, of inward-burning desire for great love. Oh most generous soul of mine, what more could you wish for? You are my one and only soul, full of the one and only godhead and the wondrous trinity. Oh purest soul of mine, what more could you desire? I am delivering three thousand souls from purgatory tonight, including Brother Jacob's soul, because of your love. These souls should have otherwise stayed in purgatory for three hundred and fifty more years. Love has liberated them from purgatory. You shall rejoice to see them in the wondrous light of eternity."

Now note how severe her ailments were. During the night she prayed to God with great earnestness for the three thousand souls and for Brother Jacob's soul. The loving God granted her wish with joy in the noble light of celestial contemplation, for in the light she saw great wonders. For example, she saw how the holy angels came in great crowds to fetch those souls from purgatory. With great noise and cheerful song they led the lovely citizens to the court of the celestial king. Our dear Lord, together with the heavenly host, received them with love and joy. Then he said with his sweet mouth: "Come, you blessed of my Father, and possess the kingdom that has been prepared for you since the beginning of the world." This was an oversweet voice, full of solace.

Then she saw that our Lord seated each soul according to her worthiness, and he said the following: "I am a good shepherd, the good shepherd and sweet bridegroom am I. I have led my sheep onto the celestial pasture, into the green-blossoming paradise, and into the angelic choir, and into the ineffable light of my godhead, and into the glory of my humanity; and I have joined them to the righteous love of my Father, and to the mildness of the Holy Spirit; and I have given them eternal peace in which they shall see me unmediated—God and human—in my perfect beauty. There they shall have a pure vision of the eternal Word. There a thousand years are like one day that has gone by yesterday."

In this light God said to her, "Out of love I will make you suffer even more than you have done so far, and you will suffer with patience according to my will." This happened as soon as it was said. God inflicted her with a wondrously great ailment that lasted for ten hours and that struck her sometimes more and sometimes less at day and at night. The suffering lasted until after compline, when the nuns go to sleep. First she fainted. Next, all of her limbs trembled and her body shook until her limbs ached and went numb. Then her heart burst. One could even hear a deep cracking sound repeatedly coming from her chest. This sounded in every respect as if the body was dying and wretchedly passing away. Finally she lowered her head and all her limbs lay lifeless for a while. She clenched her teeth tightly. Not one vein in her body pulsed or even stirred. Her eyes were wide open. She did not even seem to breathe, as I myself have tested and verified. Everyone who was there attested that they had never seen a more gruesome death than the one she was suffering then. I, the Brother who is writing this, was also present. As long as it lasted—that is, before she came to her senses—I was reminded of the sorrowful trembling of dear Jesus, which he had suffered on the cross and which shook the entire earth.

Yet while the infirmity lasted, her soul—more specifically, the highest faculty of the soul or inner human[1]—had been in a state of abundantly sweet desire, as she told me herself. During that period and until matins heaven was opened to her. Then her infirmity diminished and her soul was bathed in a celestial light. She was then unified with God in love and blissful joy, as is written about below. Also written about below are both the illness and the glorious gifts that God granted her during her infirmities.

The gentle God did even more than purge her body and soul from all sins in order to prepare for himself a well-pleasing dwelling place: he wanted to discipline her according to his will and, through love, make her a compensation for his martyrdom so that she could offer sacrifice in praise of God and for the improvement of many people—that is, that she could be useful and helpful for Christendom. Consequently, God gave her this ailment out of love. He then removed the ailment at the time which he had announced before.

58

On the day of Saint Catherine[1] he said to her, "Rejoice, my beautiful bride, sweet flower of my heart. I rejoice in all your limbs. In your soul and in all your limbs I work the deeds of high love through the unification of your will with my godhead, and with the pure knowledge of my godhead, and with eternal wisdom in which you cannot be wronged. You are a celestial column of the living and the dead. The living you heal lovingly before me as I have lovingly redeemed them on the cross with my precious blood and my Father's power. Yet the dead you constantly redeem from purgatory through your suffering."

Afterward the Lord spoke the following words: "My wisdom and clarity are enclosed within me in eternal joy, freedom, and sweet peace, and abundant bliss. I propose to create an eternal bond to all of you[2] so that you may praise me in eternity. Furthermore you shall recognize my wondrous wonders which I work incessantly through my saints. In me all things are perfected and concluded."

59

On the feast day of the Presentation of the Blessed Virgin Mary[1] the Lord said to her, "Oh chosen bride of my heart, what more could you desire? You have the high-meaning love. Oh my soul, what more could you desire? You have reached into my highest throne, that is my honor, and high imperial stream,[2] and the stream of sweet love. The latter has flowed through your soul, and it lowers you consistently into my divinity; and the power of your love flows back into me. This is the water of high love and the stream of all the saints, which always flows without interruption. Into this stream you are lowered with the sweetest delight. Oh my soul, hear my voice and keep my word. You shall let go of God for the sake of God;[3] this is my highest will and your highest reward, and it does justice to great love."[4]

60

On the feast Day of Saint Nicholas[1] the loving God, the sweet comforter of all grieving hearts, said to the soul with desire and longing, as a bridegroom does to his very dearest bride, "Oh holiest soul of mine, rejoice and rejoice. Your very dearest bridegroom comes to you, and he seeks intimacy with you, and he pours himself fully into you with a divine infusion of all that is good. So I unify you with me in blissful wholeness so that you may become one spirit with me. With ineffable joy you are lowered into the eternal Word." This means a unification with the Holy Spirit.

61

On the feast day of the Nativity of Christ the true sun of Christ and the glow of the paternal heart illuminated her heart. God was ready to prepare a delightful dwelling place in her for himself; and he spoke thus to her soul, "Oh very best soul of mine, rejoice and rejoice in the great love, because the sustainer of the world dwells in you. You are my most beloved, and my loveliest dwelling place is in you. You are the ark in which I am contained. I am a bright star shining in you, never to go down. I am the glow of the eternal light against which all lights are but darkness. In this same light you are illuminated. I am a mirror of the pure clarity in which your soul is illuminated; and in this light it sees my magnificent marvels. You are dead to yourself, living eternally in me with exultant and spiritual joy and with great jubilation of eternal love."[1]

62

Now note how with great desire she turned her heart toward God. In the same night she desired to hear the Christmas mass,[1] and her heart was filled with ardent desire and burning love.

"Suddenly heaven was opened to me, and milk and honey were flowing both in heaven and on earth. Then, through God's hand, my soul was filled with a divine infusion and with all spiritual joy. Then my lover sang to my soul with a cheerful voice this song: 'My companion, turn to me that we may look at you. Your voice is sweet in my ears and your face is beautiful.'[2] Then my soul said to him with great joy, 'My soul failed when my love spoke to me.'[3] So his image is pressed onto my heart with a unique and burning love, which is impossible to extinguish."

63

Of unspeakable ailments that she suffered on the day of the Holy Innocents.[1] "On the day of the Holy Innocents my heart was burning inwardly with a powerful love, as if it were going to burst with love. At this my beloved spoke within me: 'The infirmities you have suffered from the Feast of All Saints until now, both internally and externally—internally in your heart due to strong love and externally in fainting—shall be increased from today onward. Internally and externally they will last for more than nine weeks and be so severe that all your limbs shall tremble and crack. Your limbs shall suffer even more greatly than hitherto for the sake of my love; this is my will. With this illness you shall compensate me in a loving and thankful way for my martyrdom that I have suffered for you and for the whole world.'"

All this happened in the way God had announced. Very soon she was taken ill; her heart and body failed so badly that everyone who saw it was amazed—the same as described before. Divine love overpowered her with such great and virile strength, and with such delightful sweetness, and with such great love, that her heart was no longer able to retain the fullness of ineffable love: her heart expanded visibly because of the divine oversweetness of the heart's motion, and it thrusted upward within the body. And the distress which the heart suffered because of divine heat stretched from her heart into her arms so that she spread out all her limbs. She remained immobile and in an unnatural position as if stiffened. This lasted until Saint Agnes Day.[2]

"In spiritual contemplation I saw into the divine light. I saw three veins overflowingly running forth from God. And God the Lord said to me, 'This is the blood with which you manage to sustain many people here on earth and with which you deliver many souls from purgatory.'"

The entire heavenly host rejoiced on that same day, when her body lay stricken while the soul was engaged with sweet love. At that time her soul was led through the nine angelic choirs and before the Holy Trinity. Then he enclosed her in his divine heart. There her soul contemplated itself and saw how she was clothed with a red gown. At this, the one who loved her said to her, "Oh my very dearest soul, I have ennobled you with my precious blood, and I have adorned you with my pure godhead, and I have nourished you with the sweetness of the Holy Spirit."

Then her beloved approached her and crowned her with four crowns: firstly with the crown of justice, then with the crown of divine virtues, then with the crown of divine wisdom, then with the crown of divine love. Behold how perfectly she was adorned with all virtues and how fervently she was received into divine love. Therefore he has promised her the fellowship of the nine angelic choirs so that she may remain perpetually praising him with an incessant heat of love, together with the fiery angels.

In addition he has promised her the reward which all saints receive, when he said to her soul on Thursday after Saint Agnes Day, "Oh loving soul of mine, rejoice. You are a clear light before my eyes. After this life I will open the nine choirs of fiery angels to you. I will give you the full reward which martyrs receive and the joy of all the saints and all the angels, and in the choir of the burning seraphim you shall possess the worthiness of all the virgins."

"At that time, I had a sweet desire for my sweetest bridegroom as he said to me, 'My child, confide your suffering boldly to me. This very day you shall experience a trembling in all your limbs the same way my humanity trembled on the holy cross for the sake of humankind. And this shall happen to you at the same time of day.'" It happened thus. From sext until none[3] she suffered unspeakable trembling, all her limbs failed, and her heart burst with great love. This was in every respect comparable to a harsh death, as described before.

During this time her soul was enraptured into the ninth choir, where her worthiness, which she would own eternally, was revealed to her. Then her soul was crowned with a crown containing twelve stones which resembled twelve stars.[4] Then the chosen bridegroom and his mother sang this loving praise to her in one sweet voice: "I am giving you the assurance of eternal life and persistence until the end."[5]

64

On the feast day of Purificatio beatae Mariae[1] the Lord said to her soul in a comforting way, "Oh most generous soul of mine, rejoice. The king on the celestial throne loves you and takes pleasure in all your limbs. I, your God, work within your soul the noble works of high love with renewed joy, as I do in heaven. And I cannot turn my face from you, for I have found a dwelling place in you according to my will. The love within you is the well of all virtues. You spread your love into the whole world, for the living and the dead. Therefore you shall receive their reward and worthiness. You are a scent of my wisdom. My will is perfectly fulfilled in you."

On the Thursday after the feast day of Candlemas[2] the devout soul was in her contemplation. Consider how God comforted her in her suffering as he said, "Rejoice, my daughter, that the immortal God has become mortal for you. Your pain is joy for me. Your toil is peace for me. Your poverty is wealth for me. Your shame is honor for me. Your death is life for me."

Then on Friday he spoke to her again: "Oh my soul, rejoice. I share your toil because you suffer with me for all Christendom. Because of your virtuous life you are united with me here on earth. Therefore you shall be seated very close to me in heaven as my bride. Your love is worthy of the wounds I have suffered night and day in my limbs.[3] Six thousand three hundred and seventy-two wounds are flowing with generosity, sweetness, love, and mercy."

"On the next Sunday, great love lifted up my soul before God. As my soul was unified with God in sweet enjoyment, the beloved of my soul sang this song: 'Rejoice through the nine angelic choirs, which reside in you through my presence. I am truly resurrected in you. You have fulfilled my will with all virtues in a sacred way. With your blood and your body you have suffered for the whole world on account of my love, as I have suffered in great love for you. Heaven and earth rejoice in your torment. You dwell in the groundless depths of the Holy Trinity.'"

65

They[1] witnessed the boundless and unspeakable illness she suffered for her convent and for all sinners; as he said to her on the day of Saint Valentine, "Rejoice, my delicate dove. You shall suffer great pain from love. I am with you and will help you to carry your burden. You shall tremble for this convent and for all sinners as my humanity trembled on the cross for the whole world. You are worthy of the seven flowing rivers of my blood in which you constantly dwell." His blood flows sevenfold because it has banished the seven mortal sins. The trembling began immediately and in such a way as was described before. After her heart had burst, her soul was lowered into a divine light and she was unified with God in intimate and delightful love. "Then I experienced ineffable comfort with God.

"Then he said to me, 'Oh my chosen soul, you shall endure your toil happily through me because the force of my godhead fulfils my will in you. As my humanity trembled on the cross, so shall you tremble for five hours on account of love. As a consequence one shall hear all your limbs cracking. Oh my blessed soul, as I have suffered for you out of love, so you are patiently suffering many dreadful things for me. Therefore I will lift you up to eternal life to gain a very high reward.'

"And the Lord spoke to me again: 'Oh honorable soul of mine, rejoice. You who are ennobled and adorned with the gold of my magnificent love, you are clothed with the white ivory of my humanity and with my absolute humility. For the sake of my love you shall tremble and grow weak for three hours for the whole world, and for all souls in purgatory, and for all sinners, as I trembled for the world on the trunk of the cross. All saints, all angels, and all spirits rejoice in your torment and are in awe of it. You shall be a queen in my kingdom.'"

Consequently she suffered unspeakable ailments of body and heart. As gold is refined in the fire,[2] so was she totally purified—inwardly and outwardly—through her great love and patience, which she suffered for the whole world. Yet all her ailments and infirmities were turned into a vast sweetness.

Then he said to her, "Oh bright-shining soul of mine, my beautiful dove, you are impeccable. Because of my love you shall tremble and grow weak for two hours, as my humanity trembled on the cross. You, my dear bride, are suffering for the whole world and for all souls, as I have suffered for the whole world out of love. You, my companion, are a champion who has triumphed with me as I have triumphed on the cross. My Father's will was fulfilled through me and my will is fulfilled through you. The suffering caused by your trembling shall end today. Oh my soul, I have lifted you up—in soul and body—into a divine light and into the love of the Holy Spirit, so that all your works and exercises may be drawn into the burning fire of the divine sun, which shall never be extinguished in your soul. I give myself to you according to your will."

66

Then on Sunday Invocavit[1] he spoke once more to her soul, "Rejoice, love me, and praise me. Oh daughter of Zion, chosen bride of God, what more could you wish for? Heaven and earth are full of the greatness of your love and your worthiness. Oh my soul, I have elevated you above the nine angelic choirs. You are divinely lowered into the celestial nuptials, into the sweetness of my gentle godhead."

67
———

Of the seven joys of the Blessed Virgin Mary,
which God has revealed to her[1]

On the feast of the Annunciation of Mary[2] the Lord once more spoke to her, saying: "Oh highest soul of mine, rejoice. My heart loves you. I am in my Father, and you are in me and I am in you."

"While I was in this light God revealed to me the seven joys. The first is that her Son's perfect honor is the only thing to exceed the honor of angels and of saints. The second is that she is elevated above the angelic choirs and closest to the Holy Trinity. The third joy is this: as the day is illuminated by the sun, so the celestial court rejoices in the clarity of her presence. The fourth joy is that all the citizens of the celestial court honor and venerate her in particular, because she is the Mother of the highest king. The fifth joy is that the will of the Holy Trinity is united with her will. Anything she wills is also in perfect union with the will of the Holy Trinity. The sixth joy is that she rewards those who serve her according to her heart's desire. The seventh joy is that she can be absolutely certain that her perfect joys shall never be taken away from her, nor shall they be diminished."

68

On Passion Sunday he once more spoke to her in an amicably and loving colloquy of sweet words.[1] He said to her soul, "Oh strongest soul of mine, rejoice. My companion, I have purified you in my love, and you shall live in my love always and forever. In a high and contemplative love I have given myself to you. You have a perfect . . ."[2] "Oh very dearest soul of mine, what more could you desire? You dwell in the taste of divine sweetness; there you are strengthened with the internal sweetness of my godhead."

On Dominica in passione[3] he again spoke kind words to her, as he said to her soul, "Oh strongest soul of mine, rejoice. My companion, I have purified you in my love. In my love you shall live always and forever."

69

In cena domini dixit iterum ad animam,[1] "Oh most venerable soul of mine, rejoice. My companion, you now possess the place of bountiful grace, which sanctifies you here as well as eternally in my Father's kingdom. In a brilliant and sweet way you have concealed me in the highest delight. My soul, what more could you now wish for? Your love burns like the seraphim. My will is that your[2] will shall ever more diminish. All your distress shall have a good ending."

70

On the day of the Resurrection of the Lord[1] twelve thousand souls were redeemed through her efforts.

"Oh my most beautiful soul, rejoice. You are an adorned kingdom, in which I happily rest and blissfully dwell. You have received from me the fire of divine ardor. Your love's motion reaches into me and you melt within me from divine sweetness. You are the bread of divine love, which nourishes me. You are a vessel of all virtues, from which I drink. You are an arc of mercy, in which I—God and human—dwell, with lucid light and eternal love, as in my heavenly kingdom. This night I will free twelve thousand souls from purgatory: you have delivered them with the toil of your suffering and the trembling of your limbs. They ought to remain in agony for two thousand three hundred years, but through your love all of them are delivered. You shall be rewarded together with all of them, and you shall behold them with joy in the mirror of the Holy Trinity."

71

On the day of the Ascension of the Lord[1] he said to her, "Most noble soul of mine, rejoice. I am the path you walk into the inner sweetness of my godhead. In there you are taught all truth, and subsequently you are enraptured with purity, and you behold my Father's will. I have given you the clarity which my Father gave me, so that we may be unified. My Father is in me and I am in you and you are in us. All that I have is yours, and what you have is mine."

72

On Pentecost[1] the Lord said to her soul, "Oh very powerful soul of mine, rejoice. My companion, I sustain you in my brilliant godhead. Your heart is a house full of light and your soul is a temple full of my divinity. You are a living book with the sign of the Holy Trinity. With the seven gifts of the Holy Spirit you are sealed within the Holy Trinity."[2]

73

On the day of Saint John the Baptist[1] the Lord spoke once more to her soul: "Oh most beautiful soul of mine, rejoice. My companion, you are my blessed dwelling place, which I have chosen for myself among my saints. I constantly rest in you with my joys, as I do in heaven; and therefore I, Jesus Christ, am your dear bridegroom. You are a rose among the martyrs because of your suffering. You shall carry your virgin's crown with special worthiness.

"Oh very dearest soul of mine, what more could you desire? You are united with me in divine love, in the abyss of my divine love and ineffable grace. You flow with overflowing love. I am in you, and you shall remain in me for ever and ever."

74

Now note with what great honor and worthiness God elevated her in her soul before the entire heavenly host, as he said to her on the feast of Saint Mary Magdalene:[1] "Oh most desirable soul of mine, rejoice forever with soul and body in my divine glory. Within your precious soul you reflect my divine glow. The divine stream of love of the highest sweetness is so strong within you that every spirit marvels at the depth of the ineffable goodness that is enclosed within you.

"Oh blessed soul of mine, what more could you desire? I have placed my throne in you, and you are the throne which I occupy. Your will is united with my will."

Oh what great sweetness and consolation she felt in that union; these things, which God revealed to her in this life, are impossible to utter with a human tongue.

75

Then he said the following to her in Assumptione beatae Mariae virginis:[1] "Oh most generous soul of mine, rejoice. You have the angelic life in your soul's clarity; and you possess the jewel of your joys, the crown of your glory, and the treasure of the highest goodness. Within you dwells the abundant, honorable, and delightful bliss. Oh blessed soul, what more could you desire? You perfectly know me, and you look into the mirror of divine truth. In this mirror you greet me with friendly intimacy, and I greet you with my tender sweetness in the brilliant Trinity. In the honor of my divinity, my unique soul, you are full of the light of my sweetness, and you are high in perfection."

76

While the mass was sung on the day of the Beheading of Saint John,[1] she was alone in the infirmary as she was supposed to bandage her five wounds, which pained her enormously. This made her think of her bridegroom's five wounds, which he had suffered for her on the Holy Cross. She boldly offered the sacrifice of the pain of her wounds to his wounds, freely willing to suffer the misery for him gladly. At this sacrifice God comforted her in such a way that pain and bitterness were turned into divine sweetness. God, the true comforter of troubled hearts, did so by bringing her his holy communion himself and putting it with his own hands into her mouth and into her soul.

Then he said to his dear bride, "Rejoice, my soul, for you truly have me within you. You are one of those that my Father granted me. I will teach you the way of my life, which is the following: suffering scorn with patience, bearing destitution with wisdom, and upholding a clear conscience with strict watchfulness. So you shall have a heart of burning love. This is my will and thus was my life, which shall dwell in your heart forevermore.

"Oh my darling soul, what more could you desire? You have received me as I was received in Jerusalem. Your sustainer and your God, a king above all kings, your prince, a prince above all princes, has glorified you greatly. Your being has gone out from the magnificent worthiness of the highest one. Therefore I have clothed you with the red velvet of divine love, which everlastingly prevents you from committing any mortal sin. Oh my soul, recognize your beauty and your worthiness. You are clothed with the white velvet of complete chastity of body and soul. This is the robe that pleases me on you and that I like very much. Oh most beautiful soul of mine, rejoice. You have the sweetness of the highest virtue; therefore you are clothed with the true velvet of righteous humility, which is kindled in all of your thoughts and deeds. Humility is the virtue that took me from my Father's lap and brought me into the world, for it is the virtue on which my spirit desires to rest. Oh my soul, because you are so virtuously clothed I will rest in you eternally."

Oh what a great delight and pleasure God took in dwelling in her soul, as is proven with his words: "I delight in being with my human children, but even more in being with a well-adorned soul which has been decorated with the highest virtues."

This soul was guaranteed these virtues, as he told her: "Oh most generous soul of mine, rejoice. I take great comfort in you. The Word of the eternal Father is united with you; enjoy this union eternally, by grace in this life, and later when you will see him face to face in heaven as you wish. Oh gentle soul of mine, I grant you strong faith and true confidence, holy wisdom and spiritual desire. Oh most beloved soul of mine, I grant you justice and prudence, spiritual strength and steadfastness, as long as you live. Oh loving soul of mine, I grant you chastity and pure innocence toward all living beings so that nothing you see, hear, or consider—even if it is itself contrary to innocence—may harm you nor stain the innocence of your soul; because you shall remain in the innocence in which I have created all living beings. Oh chosen soul of mine, I grant you perfect humility, complete loyalty, and true patience until the end of your life. Oh dear soul of mine, you are clothed with all virtues."

77

On the eve of All Saints,[1] because she suffered greatly from her ailment, our Lord consoled her tenderly according to his loyal habit so that all her limbs were strengthened and overpoured with divine grace and with special sweetness. At the same time, our Lord said to her, "Do not allow your hardship to anguish you. I am as fully in you as I am in angels and saints."

Truly, it seemed to her as if her God and lover were in her. Then she desired from God—expressing this desire too—a reward for her great pain, and so she demanded five thousand souls.

78

Then on the morning of All Saints, as she received our Lord with deep desire, her heart and soul rejoiced and were filled with sweetness by love. It seemed to her that even if her heart were a mountain it would burst with sweetness, for no human tongue may speak of that sweetness.

In this sweetness and in the light of union the one who loved her said to her soul the following words: "Oh very strongest soul of mine, rejoice. Your life is in union with my life: you love me in the highest with complete perfection. You are my one and only soul. You are tortured through my love and you thirst for the draught of my love. Therefore I will give you to drink from the love of all living beings, all good people on earth, and all saints and angels in heaven. The love of all of these I will give to you that you may love me with all their love."

Yet this did not satisfy her soul. So he said to her, "Oh very tender soul of mine, I will send you into the depths of the sea— that is, into the abyss of the love of the Holy Trinity—where I will give you to drink of my love, my will, gifts, mercy, and internal as well as external virtues. This is how I provide for you in eternity."

Afterward her spirit (her intellect)[1] was lifted above itself into the Trinity, and a magnificent light came upon her soul. In this light many hidden wonderworks of our Lord were revealed to her. "Among other things I saw that everyone who is chosen stood before God the Lord, each one positioned according to their reward."

Then her soul was unified with God, and it seemed to her as if she and God were alone in heaven, with no one else present.

Because of the ineffable union of her spirit with God, it seemed to her that she were God with God and that God willed whatever she willed. Then her soul was resting in her bridegroom's arms, unmediated.[2] All of her external senses were asleep. The rest was full of sweetness, and it was so lovely that her soul had great joy and beheld great secrets of the wonderful godhead, such that it was impossible to speak to anyone about what she saw.

Then in the ensuing night the Lord said to her soul, "Oh chosen soul of mine, demand of me whatever you wish. My heart is open to you. I am defeated by your love. I cannot deny you anything. Five thousand souls I am liberating tonight from purgatory on account of your love, and I will give them my Father's kingdom forever. They should have otherwise continued to do penance in purgatory for another five hundred years."

She did not understand this to mean that each single soul should have remained in purgatory for five hundred years, rather that each soul had a particular sentence to serve according to its sins, and the sum of their time to serve equaled five hundred all together.

"Because you have delivered them through your love, you shall receive special worthiness and own the eternal life together with them.

"Oh blossoming, most beautiful, and holiest soul, chosen dove of mine, you shall be elevated into the ninth angelic choir. What more could you desire? The highest love is a fortification of virtue grounded in your heart. Your worthy soul is a bond of perfection and blessedness to my eyes. Grace gives you that which I have by nature. All this, gentle soul, you shall share with us in the highest truth."

79

On the following Holy Christmas he spoke once more to her: "Oh wonderful soul of mine, rejoice. You enter blessedly into my pure divinity in the heavenly paradise, where you shall perpetually behold my Father's face unimpeded by sin. Oh brilliant soul of mine, as free as an eagle you may fly into the highest height and into the gracious face of the eternal godhead, while your soul's clear eyes are strengthened in the reflection of the eternal divine sun."

80

Starting on the eve of Epiphany[1] and lasting throughout the night and the day, she suffered such great agony and pain of heart and body that all her limbs shuddered and failed her: it seemed that no human had ever died such a gruesome death. She died as wretchedly in heart and body as that time on All Saints Day— back then it had occurred every night for three hours over twelve days, with manifold torments and severe and constant fainting of her mind;[2] such a thing had never been known to have happened to any human.

I—who am writing this—saw with my own eyes that she suffered such pain, agony, and impotence, and such shuddering of the limbs, dying and reviving, that no tongue could possibly or adequately speak about it. This is because it went too far against nature's course: no force of nature can have this effect on a human. But God alone wanted to work in her and through her with his divine might. Go look up[3] how all-consuming the pain and dying was, and also why God imposed it on her. You will find it all written on All Saints Day in the year before this one.[4] There you may read of a similar shuddering, trembling, and dying.

But regarding what I myself witnessed, she said the following words to me: "During this torment my soul was flooded and illuminated with divine love, and my spirit hovered in God. And it seemed to me as if he were present within me and as if I gently forced my lover to join my soul so that I could gladly behold him, fly to him with an illuminated heart and soul, and cleave my soul to him with graciousness and thirst. I entirely entrust him with my soul as he entirely loves me.

"In the light and love, my heart—and my intellect—was lifted up to contemplate and to recognize divine things. My desire was kindled to know and to taste how much sweeter than sweet my lover is. I had marvelous and intimate joy with the friends of God—the God who defeats any enemy. As my soul was elevated into the light of pure knowledge, up above human nature, my body too was elevated through God's power. My body was elevated seven times, which the members of the convent and the others who were with me witnessed. Divine love and fervent desire; these two draw my soul together so that it becomes drunk on the overflowing inpouring of the Holy Spirit, in which I confidently rest.

"Sometimes he appears to me in a rapture, like a ray of divine light. Then he enraptures my spirit above itself, as I now yearn to see God as in a mirror.[5] Human prudence[6] fails now, because I sleep sweetly in the contemplation of God and in the arms of my gentle bridegroom. During this time he reveals to my sight many things that are hidden in God. No one is able to take from me the joy and the purity of divine grace that I have now tasted. The divine glow, the light, pours itself into me, and combines itself with me, making of two—that is, of my soul and of God—one spirit; and my soul becomes God with God, fully unified with

God. This unification only ever happens in the greatest heat of love and in the very sweetest desire of love. This makes my soul melt everywhere; and it becomes soft, unlike its usual stiffness; and my soul becomes susceptible to the fire of the Holy Spirit and flows like melted wax into the divine image—which it had seen in the rapture of its intellect—and it is shaped in the image of the imprint. No human can get there by his own effort. Only the Holy Spirit, in his light and in his love, can enrapture the human to that place, where all human power is silenced and calmed, where God's power alone is active. Although the soul is created solely in order to know God, it cannot transcend itself all by itself, but needs to be divinely elevated by him in whose likeness it is created. This is the natural worthiness of living beings with an intellect. By itself the soul cannot comprehend divine things, but it can receive divine things if God helps it. No living beings are capable of this other than those that are made in God's image, because they are drawn to God. This union is the soul's highest perfection in this life."

During the union of her soul with God, her lover said the following words to her soul: "Hey divine soul of mine, rejoice for ever and ever, and sing my name, which I have grounded in you.[7] You are formed after the image of the Holy Trinity, adorned with my likeness. You are betrothed to me as a bride in eternity; this is in good faith, since I have redeemed you with my precious blood.

"Oh blessed soul of mine, you are destined to dwell eternally with the holy angels. You may grasp in me the bliss of all the saints. You are an heir of my eternal godhead and a partaker in the threefold unity.

"What more could you desire? Your soul and my heavenly kingdom—which is in you—are adorned with stars, moon, and sun.[8] The stars, which adorn the soul, are flowering[9] virtues. The moon is the pure faith in Christ, together with righteous confidence. The sun is the righteous and burning love for God and for your neighbors." In this way God turned her soul into the firmament[10] and adorned her with all the virtues.

In the same light, her beloved furthermore said to her soul, "My soul, I have crowned you with five great virtues: divine love, wisdom, righteousness, modesty, and fortitude." In this way her soul will have joy upon joy in the Holy Spirit at all times, forever, without end.

81

On Saint Agnes Day[1] her soul and heart had ineffable joy as well as the sweet grace of the one who loved her. It seemed to her that his might and his sweetness flowed so abundantly into her soul that she felt a great heat of burning love; and so she thought that her soul had divinely become God with God. She also had a clear perception of being perfectly formed in the image of God.

In this state of clarity she saw that God had crowned her soul with a golden crown, in which were set three large precious stones. The entire celestial court especially enjoyed and praised the crown's beauty. The first stone contained in the crown symbolized[2] the joy that she had especially in the divinity and humanity of our dear Lord. The second stone symbolized the joy that she had from the Mother of God. The third stone symbolized the joy that her soul in particular had from all the saints and all the angels. In addition to this crown, our dear Lord gave her soul a wedding band as a sign of righteous love and total union—which God and her soul then secretly shared—so that they would never be separated.[3] Her soul was in this light and in this grace at all times, day and night.

"Oh lovely soul of mine, rejoice. You are my throne, made of ivory,[4] which is the only throne that I want to rest on. My companion, what more could you wish for? The Holy Spirit works four lovely things in you: your face is splendidly reflected in the impeccable mirror of my godhead; your temper is well balanced; your heart is full of divine love; your soul is full of ardent desire. You are my companion, my dove, my sister, my bride.[5] What more could you now desire? I have erected your love in righteous humility, I have confirmed it with patience, and I have perfected it with steadfast love. Your life is a rose blooming[6] before my godhead."

82

On the day of Saint Gregory[1] her soul was in a state of great sweetness and it was unified with God. During this union her soul desired that God would direct it onto a virtuous path as he most lovingly willed. Our dear Lord then said to her soul, "Love me, and fear me, and fulfill my will in all things. Whatever you need—whether bodily necessities or spiritual consolation—I will never deny you."

A state of great sweetness lasted in her soul from matins until noon, and all the while it seemed to her that love's sweetness was so great that her soul was fully unified with God, and that her soul and God were alone in the heavenly kingdom. It also seemed to her that no one else other than herself was left on earth, and that she was nothing else than one will with God. During this period, it seemed to her soul that it was lowered so deeply into the might, wisdom, and grace of God that it could do or not do anything she wanted, as if she were God within God. Because of her soul's sweetness her human nature failed as if she were going to die right then. Then God gave her soul the ability to pull down into itself the one who loved her, doing so with boundless joy and joyful sweetness.[2]

"Oh most praiseworthy soul of mine, rejoice; because from the abyss of my heart, you draw the immensely sweet taste and holiness of my divine love, which makes you forget all ephemeral things; because with a pure heart you fly above yourself and into my pure godhead, where your soul is divinely illuminated and where it is instructed with divine sweetness, with highest perfection."

83

On Easter, as this devout virgin once more performed her habitual prayer and devotion for souls, the sweet Lord said to her soul, "Oh honorable soul of mine, what more could you desire? You are overly beautiful, pure, and wholly chaste. Your purity is within me, together with the clarity of your heart. By having perfected the virtue of contemplation you are entirely lowered into my love. With the eyes of your soul, you look into the marvelous mirror of the Holy Trinity, into the very dearest will of my Father.

"Oh blessed soul of mine, what more could you desire? Tonight I am freeing two thousand souls from purgatory. They should have remained in purgatory for five hundred years, but the force of your love has redeemed them from all their pain and has cleansed them from all the stains of their sins. These souls shall especially glorify, reward, and honor you, with the thank-fulness they hold for each other.[1] All of this, my soul, you shall receive in the mirror of divine worthiness."

84

On the day of Ascensio Domini[1] he spoke once more to her: "Unconquerable soul of mine, what more could you desire? You do the works of charity. Therefore the abyss of the well called the Holy Trinity is unlocked to you, that you may draw from it as much as you can hold in yourself and then equally pass it on to others. You, my companion, may help them to understand their sins through your suffering; and afterward, my dove, you may obtain mercy for them with your love; furthermore, with your patience you may serve them as a good example; and with your words and deeds you may give them good teaching. Oh soul of mine, you are the one whom I have chosen according to my heart's desire. Therefore my will shall be wholly fulfilled in you."

85

On Holy Pentecost,[1] as she was in great sweetness and fervent love, God the Lord said to her soul, "Oh holy soul of mine, rejoice. You are the pinnacle of perfected virtues. Oh brilliant love and pure soul of mine, what more could you desire? I am a fire incessantly burning in your heart, which illuminates you sweetly and kindles you tenderly. Oh tender soul of mine, what more could you desire? I am the font of clemency, the praise of angels, the honor of saints. You are transformed in me and I pour my divine stream into you.

"Oh blessed queen, you special joy of angels, and special jewel of women and of all the saints, rejoice.[2] You have embraced eternal bliss, in which your will is wholly fulfilled and which gladly brings mercy to your soul. I have embraced your soul with my divine honor, and I have enraptured all your senses into the purity of inner sweetness. There your heart is illuminated with the highest love and with wisdom.

"Oh sweet soul of mine, rejoice. I am truly in you and I confirm to you that you shall never part from me again.[3] My delightful dwelling place is in you. Oh blessed soul of mine, what more could you desire? You seek me with a sweet, happy, and dignified song; and you find me anytime in sweet love, according to your heart's desire; and you receive me in divine sweetness with strong thirst; and you enjoy me blissfully with sweet affection[4]—the affection of blessed blessedness, in which is enclosed all that is good. Oh gentle soul of mine, what more could you desire? I longingly surrender myself to you in total love so that you may enjoy the loving delight of my divine nature, in which is enclosed the highest good."

86

On the day of Saint Mary Magdalene[1] he spoke once more to her soul, "Oh holy soul of mine, rejoice. Your whole life is a divine life. You desire perfectly in pure love. Oh my soul,[2] my heart is wholly inclined to you. What else could you desire, since in the highest heaven of the wisdom of inward purity you have held the treasure of your bridegroom's worthiness? My love within you is a peaceful salvation, a bodily power, a heartfelt gentleness, a firm freedom from ambition,[3] a high knowledge of yourself and of my godhead, and a strong thirst for sweetness. All this, my tender soul, you have found in the holy intimacy of the true love which he who solely loves you has for you; he, who ties you closely to him and instructs you wisely with spiritual joys."

87

On the feast day of Assumptio Mariae[1] he spoke with her again, saying to her soul the following words: "Oh blessed soul of mine, rejoice. You have the eternal life of all sweetness within you. Oh tender soul of mine, what more could you desire? All of your works—your life—are divine actions, which God performs through you. Therefore all the divine works I do through you are always good and directed toward the best.

"Oh dear soul of mine, what more could you wish? I teach you and I love you. The eternal divine wisdom, which kindles your heart in perfect love, all the angels and all the saints, glow and burn in the brilliance of my godhead, and your noble soul burns in steadfast love before my divine face."

88

On the day of the Nativity of the Virgin Mary[1] God the Father spoke thus to her: "Blessed soul of mine, rejoice. You have within you my only begotten Son, who is full of grace and truth.[2] For you are illuminated with grace, and truth wisely teaches you to know my will.

"Oh blessed daughter of mine, what more could you desire? In the blessed clemency of my ineffable love, I am a jewel to your soul. You are securely kept on a sweet pasture, in the blissful peace of the enjoyment of burning love. There you shall dwell eternally, without end."

89

On the feast day of the Archangel Michael[1] she was in a state of great devotion and fervent love, as he spoke to her soul: "Oh venerable soul of mine, you light of Christendom, rejoice. Since you are truly unified with me, melted because of my divine love and entirely poured into me, I am loved by your love, and you are loved by my love. Still, you love through grace, whereas I love by nature.

"Oh blessed soul of mine, what more could you wish for? Everything that I work in you, and that you see and hear within me, is nothing other than the action of the divinity, which pours out of me and into you. I endow you incessantly with the drink of the love of all the angels and all the saints; and I always live in you with renewed mercy and marvel."

90

On the day of the Eleven Thousand Virgins[1] he said to her soul, "Dear soul of mine, rejoice. You are fully united with this per-fected love and your great teaching. Oh gentle soul of mine, what more could you desire? You are fulfilled by God at all times, so that all your deeds are a pure goodness within me, and they are a divinely foreseen ordinance, which you receive from my Father. Oh my soul, what more could you desire? Your love constantly transcends itself and enters the highest good."

91

On the feast day of All Saints[1] he said to her soul the following words: "Oh highly praised soul, which is a growing blessedness through the workings of the Holy Trinity; oh tender soul of mine, what more could you desire? You are formed according to the Holy Trinity, and I, your bridegroom, am clothed with the gown of your humanity. And this will be your highest joy in heaven: that you will eternally enjoy my humanity and my divinity as you wish.

"Oh chosen soul, what more could you desire? Unfailingly observing virtues, you dwell in the mirror of my godhead; and you do so with the security of divine love, which has renewed you with ineffable joy and with eternal sweetness, which—because of my clemency—flows through you night and day.

"Oh wonderful soul, what more could you desire? Your face is lovely to me. Your love, suffering ineffable toil, has forced me to release three thousand souls from the agony of purgatory tonight. They would have remained in purgatory for three hundred and forty years, had not your love and your immense suffering paid their ransom. Therefore each of these souls will particularly glorify you in heaven."

92

On the first Sunday of Advent he once more spoke with her, saying to her soul: "Oh most generous bride of mine, rejoice. I am the life of your soul within you, the word and the wisdom of the Father, who divinely teaches you all wisdom, all virtue, and all that is good. For I remain in you, always, with perfect wisdom, mercy, and sweet instruction. For I am the highest wisdom of the utmost grace, which always blossoms in your soul and dwells in your heart.

"Oh very dearest soul of mine, rejoice. You have risen like the powerful sun to save Christendom. With the help of my godhead, you penetrate the summit of the light of the Holy Trinity, so that my joy may be in you. Oh wonderful soul, what more could you desire? You live in the high love of my divine wisdom, that is, in holy delight; in the perfection of grace; in the magnitude of a fervent and willing devotion; in the fiery love; in the sun of divine brilliance; and in the mirror of the Holy Trinity, in which you please me very well. For my will is your will, and your will is my will.

"Oh very dearest soul of mine, with this wondrous pact of special love,[1] you are divinely embraced more than all others."

93

On the feast day of Epiphany[1] he spoke once more to her soul: "Oh very dearest soul of mine, rejoice. In your noble soul you hold the high treasure of the angels' joy and the saints' sanctity, and it cannot be stolen from you. You are confirmed in my godhead.

"Oh dear soul of mine, what more could you wish for? With great liberty, you fly on the high path into my pure godhead. Therefore I will elevate you among my angels and saints, and I will give you a place in ineffable glory."

94

Later, on the feast day of Purificatio Mariae,[1] her soul was in great devotion and in fervent love, as the lovely God once more spoke to her soul with honeyed words.

"Oh most radiant soul of mine, rejoice. You are a flower of my saints in my eternity. You are a sweet fruit of my saints. In the Holy Trinity I have made you equal to a white lily among my virgins. Oh my soul, what more could you desire? You recognize me clearly in all things. You love me constantly and purely, which means you love me solely for my own sake. You love me boundlessly and you enjoy me as you wish.

"Oh my bride, be content. You have a celestial body and an angelic soul. Oh most gentle soul of mine, what more could you desire? I have made myself a dwelling place in you. You are a delightful garden to me,[2] and I long to be with you. So shall you eternally dwell with me in the highest joy. There you shall see the beauty of all the saints and the grandeur of all the angels; and the honor of my royal majesty, of the Father's might, of the Son's wisdom, and of the Holy Spirit's clemency. There, tender flower, you shall recognize the Holy Trinity clearly.

"Oh pure soul of mine, rejoice. I have lowered you into the depth of my godhead, from whence you draw the abundance of all abundance, the sweetness of all sweetness, and the clarity of all clarity. Oh blessed soul of mine, I have ennobled you greatly and I have loved you strongly. In addition I have chosen you in order to divinely unify my will with yours."

95

Annuntiatio Mariae[1]

"Oh ineffable soul of mine, and great concealed intimacy of my divine heart, what more could you desire? I, God and human, am within you together with grace. In my godhead you have received a blessed infusion of sweet joy; hence you are sweeter than sweet within me. And this illuminates your intellect.[2]

"Oh holy soul of mine, and great concealed intimacy of my divine heart, what more could you desire? You are a pillar of the divine temple. The whole world is blessed before my Father through your suffering and through your love. You praise me and you live with the saints in my godhead. You are a temple of God filled with sanctity.

"Oh dear soul, what more could you wish for? You are an ineffable being in the wondrous Trinity, which all saints praise, which comforts all Christian souls, and which remains unknown to all hearts. Oh blossoming fecund soul of mine, what more could you desire? You are a flower of virtue. Oh dear soul of mine, what more could you desire? In my love I fulfill your will with my high work. Oh my soul, what more could you desire? You burn with high knowledge in the godhead of my Father, in whom you are confirmed. And your will is fully united with my will. Therefore your life is praiseworthy according to the Holy Trinity.

"Oh praiseworthy soul, your heart blossoms.[3] Whatever you have poured out on account of love for me, I have received in my divine heart. I will give you my prisoners because I cannot deny anything to you. Tonight I am freeing one thousand souls from purgatory, which you have redeemed with your blood, your heavy toil, and your suffering. They should have remained in agony for three hundred years. Your loyal love alone has redeemed them. Therefore you shall be specially rewarded, together with all of them, in the mirror of the Holy Trinity.

"Oh ineffable soul of mine, what more could you desire? For I have directed your intentions according to my heart and my will, and I have ordered your intentions through revealed truth.[4] Anything you wish is likewise my will, for the sake of Virtue.[5]

Oh blessed soul, what more could you desire? Your heart blossoms with the fullest grace and your virtues blossom with holy works.[6] Your soul glows with praiseworthy love in my lovely godhead, in which you are filled with joy and sweetness in the unity of the Holy Trinity.

"Perfect soul of mine, rejoice. You have the true humility, which does not desire praise. My divine grace is concealed within your heart more than in anyone else's. Oh holy soul, what more could you desire? Inwardly you draw joy from all the virtues; that is why your heart cannot be troubled by anyone being unjust to you, whether in words or deeds. The delight that you enjoy in my godhead likewise cannot be diminished. Oh blessed soul, rejoice. By serving me—God—you have vanquished your body to the extent that it obeys the spirit, just as I wish. Oh dear soul of mine, rejoice. You keep in sweet memory the one who loves you, who in the height of his wisdom has confirmed you with his wondrous splendor. Oh my dove, rejoice. You have been given the true and high grace by your creator, and not by anything created. You have spurned all ephemeral things. Oh dear soul of mine, I am the one who loves you. Nothing may fulfil your noble soul other than the Holy Trinity, after which it is formed. Oh worthy soul, rejoice. With ardent sweetness you have drawn the knowledge of my godhead into you, within which you are united with me in marvelous intimacy and knowledge of my secret place. You are made equal to me.

"Oh blessed chaste soul, what more could you desire? You have a fertile love that no one can diminish or extinguish. Your love shines through the angelic choirs as does the sun-like brightness which is contained in my godhead. There, among the high burning seraphim, you shall forever dwell with joy. Oh precious soul of mine, rejoice. In eternity I have chosen you so that my abundant, eternal, and ineffable goodness and graciousness shall work within you to my heart's desire. Oh blessed soul, what more could you desire? My Father loves you and has shown you mercy through my intercession. And the more full you are with mercy, the more worthily you love my Father and the more he forces you to pass on mercy. Therefore I support you with the fruit of my life as a human on earth, which is the redemption of the sins of many people. Oh my dear companion, in this way your life assists the fertile reward of my humanity, which is to come and rescue humankind. And they shall be lastingly comforted by the reward of my Passion."[7]

96

"On Epiphany[1] my soul was in great grace, as it saw in a blissful light that God was a burning god, a powerful god, a glowing god, a consoling god, and a fertile god in his chosen children. And God with his burning love poured into them the stream of eternal life, so that their hearts would be kindled with love and thus become worthy before God. And he illuminated them with a divine light, so that they could recognize both their own flaws and the way of truth. And he strengthened them with his mercy. As soon as they risked failing in their spiritual strength, he poured his divine mercy and might into them, that they would be strengthened in him. And he consoled them with his divine consolation. As soon as he punished them with his paternal rod, which was too harsh for human bodies to endure, he joyfully poured into them the promise that he would give them the heavenly kingdom and himself, forever. And with his mercy he made their souls' virtues fertile, thus renewing and sweetening their lives in God.

"Once I desired to pray for a person, hoping that God would make known to me what sort of life she had. Then our Lord said: 'If my children seek to be permanently good, they shall do four things, as I shall do four things for them in return. The first: if they leave their family for me, I will give them sweet thoughts. The second: if they love their enemies for my sake, I will give them fervent love. The third is that if they eschew the praise of humans for my sake, I will give them great desire for me. The fourth: if they patiently do their work for my sake, I will give them great reward and virtue with a constant flow, and I will give myself to them as a reward, eternally. So I will have relieved them from death and given them the eternal life after this life.'"

97

On Easter God laid a magnificent light on his bride. In this light she saw how all spirits were glorified and renewed in the divine light. And all their hearts were nourished and kindled with divine light and comfort.[1]

"And God revealed to me all things in heaven and on earth. And he revealed to me all his works distinctly, because he grants everyone that which they are each able to receive. And I saw that God is everywhere; however, he is more in good people than in anyone else. And once my soul recognizes him as he is, it becomes as he is: almighty and powerful as he is. God is as sweet and generous as he wishes; and he is perceptible in taste once the soul loves him. Then it receives sweetness from God as it loves him. Therefore it loves God for God's sake. Once God joins his sweet being[2] to the soul, the soul tastes an overly delicious sweetness of God within God. That is loving God for God's sake. Yet to love oneself for God's sake is perfect. Altogether, the loving soul loves God for God's sake. It maintains a righteous love only when it does not love God for its own profit, or because it cannot do without God, but loves him solely—with his help—for his pure goodness. And once it can taste God, it ascends within God with constant strength, fiery love, and great praise. God is a consuming fire to the soul. The fire's smoke means peace in every human heart. Our peace burns in heaven, that is, in God, once all earthly things are no more than ashes and dust to us.

"As my soul was united with God in this way, on this holy Easter Day, the one who loves me said to my soul, 'Oh mirror of all good conduct, you are seated in God's peace. The Holy Trinity is your crown. Demand of me whatever you wish.'

"At this my soul demanded to convert in turn ninety-two, seven hundred, ninety thousand, and three hundred souls; and that all good people be confirmed by God. God, with his powerful love, fulfilled all this, as it was clearly revealed to me. I saw that God, through his mercy, released the aforementioned number of souls from purgatory leading them onto the celestial pasture and seating them in his perfect splendor, each one placed according to their worthiness. Then their joy flowed into God. And God loved each soul so much that he had the intimacy that he shared with them then and that he continues sharing with each single one of them, separately in eternal joy. Not even Our Dear Lady knows this joy, nor does any angel, nor any other living being; for God wishes to be with each soul as if there existed none other than God and the soul alone.

"Thus spoke the Lord to these aforementioned souls: 'Come, my dear chosen children, to the grace, which is prepared for you from the beginning of the world, for you have done my will. I shall reveal to you my royal Lordship which will end all your hardship.' They have arrived in the celestial magnificence. There God reveals to them his godhead. There they sing to him the joyful song 'Alleluia' in sweet and fine voices. The angels join their song. They all sing in unison. Their music ascends to the heavens.[3] They all proclaim: 'We praise our comforter because we were lost, but through him we were redeemed from hell's darkness. Our great hardship has ended. Therefore we honor and praise you, sweet Father and God, that we shall recognize you in the depth of your groundless godhead.'[4]

"This blessed Easter Day was a dear, sweet, happy day. At that time my soul was in a state of great grace; and God revealed to me his magnificent wonders: how he pours his mercy into good and into bad people. It also saw how he pours his blessed blood into those who protect themselves against sin.

"Then my soul asked, 'Lord, what will you do with these?'

"Our Lord answered, 'I will open my heart to them because it is wounded of love.'

"To this my soul said, 'Lord, how are you with those who love only you and who spurn all worldly things?'

"The Lord countered, 'I will seat them in the hearts of good people and I will turn their toil into a common good, abundant with love.'

"At this my soul inquired, 'Lord, what will you do with those who practice all virtues?'

"To this our Lord replied, 'I will pour my mercy into them, that they shall blossom before my face as May does at the accorded time.'

"Then I continued, 'Lord, how will you fare with those who desire to honor your Passion?'

"Our Lord returned, 'I will prepare a seat for them in my groundless godhead.'

"Next I questioned, 'Lord, what will you do with sinners?'

"To this our Lord responded, 'I am going to be with them day and night, and at all times. And I will not separate myself from them until they have fallen so deeply into sin that they trample me under their feet. At this moment I will separate myself from them, forever.'

"And our Lord said, 'Those who follow me I will guide to where I am.'

"And I saw that God poured into one person these five responses, one by one; and he does all of this in divine union and with sweet enjoyment of their soul."[5]

98

"On the feast day of Saint John the Baptist[1] my soul had great joy and bliss with God. And my soul saw and heard many wonders and much knowledge, and how God orders things; and he gave all things their beings. Yet the merriest thing of all which God gives is life itself.

"Then my soul inquired, 'Lord, what is life?'

"To this the Lord responded, 'This is the eternal life: that they recognize me and my only begotten Son whom I have sent.'

"Suddenly my soul heard the masters debating what eternal life depends on.[2]

"The first group argued, 'On knowledge.'

"The second held, 'On love.'

"The third group posited, 'On enjoyment of God.'

"God, however, reveals to my soul that one cannot love him

unless one knows him; because he whom I do not know is so far from me that I cannot love him. The better I know God, the more firmly my soul loves him. God is endless; therefore knowledge of God must be endless; as must loving God in this knowledge, and enjoyment of God in this love. In that way God proved to my soul that one without the other does not make sense, because knowing, loving, and enjoying God creates in my soul an eternal life in God. Then all things are fulfilled in God: when anything works without mediation."[3]

99

"On Corpus Christi[1] my soul was in a calmly flowing light. And in this light I saw that he is the origin of all light and the well of all life and the outpouring of all being. And all the good things that living beings may receive are nothing compared to what God—the living well—is in himself.

"And I saw that each soul is closer to God than it is to itself, and that whoever does not know God in this life shall never be able to enjoy him in the afterlife. Therefore shall a human progress from all his flaws toward a perfect being, so that the same human's inward devotion is always sufficiently maintained. At this time my soul said, 'Lord, I do everything I can. But if you want me to do more than I am able to, I will need your help.'

"Afterward my soul rested in God for three days. Once the soul is fully settled and quietened, it has rested. On the third day my soul became as bright as the sun, which means that God alone works in the soul, unmediated. Thus he truthfully worked within the soul, and it became as brilliant as truth. Nothing other than truth radiated from it.

"In this light my soul saw four baptisms. The first one washes away original sin, and this baptism purifies outwardly and inwardly. And as God was once born of Our Dear Lady, so are we all baptized, every day, in this baptism. As the angel said to the Virgin Mary, 'The Holy Spirit shall come upon you to clean your blood and flesh, and the power of the highest shall overshadow you to reflect the Father's image in you, and the Son shall touch you to form himself again in you.'[2] Hence, at this baptism the Father's voice was heard, the Son prepared the water, and the Holy Spirit was seen in the shape of a dove.[3] And the divine power flows, because of God's humanity, into the water; and so no matter how many flaws you may have, you could not therefore claim to receive less mercy.[4] This baptism happens once, but the power of the baptism and its effect happen in the soul not only once, on one day—but at all times, on all days."

100

"In annuntiatione beatae Mariae virginis[1] God gave me a great and wonderful light to behold. In this light a voice said, 'Fiat.' This is the noblest word that has ever been uttered. It means this much: An uninterrupted closeness of divine nature takes place in the unity of the three persons. This word has also been uttered at the time when the divine and human nature were united in one person. It is also uttered in unison during the union, when the soul is united with God.

"Then my soul[2] saw in the effusion—that is, the revelation—that he reveals himself; and his revealing is his speaking. In this way the soul saw the angelic spheres, which means that God speaks with them. God does not have a tongue, nor a mouth, nor anything. What then does he speak with? They say that he speaks through angels,[3] as he reveals himself to each one of them according to their rank before God. God's outpouring[4] is a blazing will amidst the light of speaking; the Son eternally flows out of the Father and keeps his nature and his person, and the Father and the Son remain with the Spirit in eternity.[5] Then all living beings are God within God amidst the effusion. Then God gives himself distinctly, first to angels, second to humans. God does all of this.

"The second 'fiat' that has ever been uttered in history occurred among the words Our Dear Lady spoke to the angel: 'Fiat mihi secundum verbum tuum.'[6] This word 'fiat,' which Our Dear Lady said, was desired by the Holy Trinity in unity. The unity is that of the Father as he has foreseen it, of the Son in whom it has been fulfilled, and of the Holy Spirit who partakes in it. And all living beings desired this word, since it was eternally foreseen in God to be said by Our Dear Lady for the salvation of humankind and in particular to honor God and all his living beings. Had the word not been said, all his doings would have been naught. This historical unification—which was eternal within God—was supposed to happen through the word that Our Dear Lady would utter. All humankind desired this to happen. However, she waited far too long before she said it. She understood well that it transcended the nature of all created things. In this light my soul saw that with the word 'fiat' Our Dear Lady conceived God bodily, in his humanity. At the same time as this word 'fiat' was said, the unification of body and soul happened; and as these two unified, the divine nature and the human nature did so in one person. As my soul saw this, it perceived inwardly and swiftly—in the very same moment—that God became human, which is why I claim that the unification and its effect occur beyond the realm of time. The angel said to Our Dear Lady, 'Ave gratia plena, dominus tecum.'[7] She did not pay much attention to these first words. The angel said that she was full of grace; and that God had constantly been spiritually with her in her soul, before God would be given a bodily birth through her; and that the divine order and his wisdom in the shape of human nature alone . . . [8] Thus this order was fulfilled. If it had been the case that she had died before our Lord could be born, she would have gone straight to limbo. Yet, had God not been so lovingly and deeply in her soul, he would never have been born from her bodily. Then I heard how angels and saints praised her because of her virtues, of which she had many because all virtues were in her, constantly and incessantly, as part of her being with God. Then I heard and saw the eternal Word: that it became flesh and that it continually flows out from the Father like a reflection.

"Were a man so big that his head reached to the sky and his feet to the abyss, and were his arms as wide as the firmament, you would still be able to see him entirely in a small mirror held in front of him. This is a metaphor for the sun. The masters say that even the smallest star among the firmament's stars is larger than the entire earth. Therefore the sun is much larger than the earth. Whoever held a small mirror toward the sun would still be able to see it entirely in the same mirror. In the same way, the eternal Word was flowing in this divine mirror; and he took on human nature—not the human person; and by the work of the Holy Spirit the body was created in the purest and most chaste blood of Mary's virginal heart;[9] and all of this happened in a short moment of time; and none of these works had ever happened before or would happen again, because only at this one instance were God and human conceived in one person. As soon as she said this word 'fiat,' the Son of God was in her virginal body. This word 'fiat' is a noble word, in which all our bliss is enclosed.

"The third 'fiat' that is spoken is—daily, in eternity, as well as in this age—with the tender soul which is united with God. In the union, the soul knows God and tastes God in divine nature. Then God shines over it as the sun shines over the moon. Then God flows into God. Then grace makes the soul into what God is by nature; and it is lowered into the groundless well of divine nature. Then it is rid of itself as God is rid of all names. So it dies in the wonders of the godhead. Then God flows into God; and the soul cannot grasp the divine nature. The soul which beholds God must be dead to all stains of sin." Etc.[10]

Notes

1. Re "nun": technically, the women in a Premonstratensian Order are not nuns but canonesses; see Schilp, *Norm und Wirklichkeit*, 90–96, 195–201. On canonesses, see also Klapp, "Negotiating Autonomy." For easier access to the text, I have decided to translate the original *cloister jonffrauwe* (*Vita*, 283) as "nun" rather than "religious woman" or "canoness." Re "in the diocese of Mainz": it is unclear what the formulation in the original, *yn Mentzer strome* (ibid.), means—perhaps "in the lands of the river Main"? More likely, though, it means the diocese of Mainz, to which the convent of Hane belonged in the Middle Ages (today the convent would be located in the diocese of Speyer). On the history and ecclesiastic organization of Hane, see Backmund, *Monasticon Praemonstratense*, 96. [N.B. In these notes, *Vita* refers to my critical edition of the *Life*, as listed under Edited and Translated Primary Sources in the reference list. References to Kirakosian, *Die Vita der Christina von Hane* concern the analytical study of the 2017 monograph.]

CHAPTER I

1. See Est 2:3–18.

CHAPTER 2

1. The word *materie* (*Vita*, 283) is here translated as "narrative," but literally it means "matter." Its use reveals a knowledge of technical vocabu-

lary regarding the composition of texts, *materie* being a term that was also employed in other medieval hagiographies to denote a narrative thread or a theological issue. See, respectively, Rapp, "Storytelling as Spiritual Communication," 432; and Backmund, *Die mittelalterlichen Geschichtsschreiber*, 90.

2. The term "heart" is used throughout the *Life* to mean either the physical organ, the mind, or the general mental state of a person. This multitude of meanings is in line with the medieval understanding of the heart as seat of the soul, as in medieval language the heart comes to represent many abstract conditions of human existence such as courage, feeling, intention, and mind; see Webb, *The Medieval Heart*. Therefore I have decided to keep "heart" in most cases rather than interpreting in each instance a specific meaning.

CHAPTER 3

1. See Lk 24:31.
2. Lk 23:32.

CHAPTER 4

1. See Ps 31:5.
2. The words *eyn stymme eyns geistlichen ynsprechs* (*Vita*, 285) are here translated as "a voice speaking spiritually and inwardly"; literally, *geistliches ynsprech* means "spiritual inspiration" or "spiritual and inner speech." The term *ynsprech* is only attested in German mystical texts of the fourteenth century.
3. The word for "vision" is *gesicht;* it appears five more times (Chs. 5, 6, 10, 25, 34).
4. See Ps 16:6.

CHAPTER 5

1. *Nativitatis Domini* (Lord's Nativity) means Christmas Day and is celebrated on December 25.
2. See Jn 20:11.

CHAPTER 6

1. The original does not have a first-person speaker in this phrase, but a passive construction ("as described before" is a literal translation) would be ambiguous.

CHAPTER 7

1. The word *meysterschen* (*Vita*, 288) is here translated as "magistra." In the lifetime of Christina of Hane, Premonstratensian women's convents were governed by so-called magistrae ("mistresses"), who correspond to prioresses; see Krings, "Die Frauenklöster in der Pfalz," 184.

2. See Mt 3:16.

CHAPTER 9

1. Historically, the convent of Hane experienced a period of poverty during Christina's lifetime; see Mittermaier, "Wo lebte die selige Christina," 79.

2. A corresponding quote attributed to Saint Gregory is not known. It is unclear which text source this quotation refers to.

3. The word *spegel* (*Vita*, 290) in the original, here translated as "paragon," means "mirror" and is used like Latin *speculum* to denote Christina's exemplary status.

CHAPTER 10

1. This is not a direct quote from the Bible but may refer to Tb 2:12.

2. Ws 3:6.

3. A besom is a type of broom made from a bundle of brushwood.

4. Exactly which saints' lives serve as model is not specified, but Saint Radegund is a possibility, since her application of fire to the body is similarly described; as her male hagiographer Fortunatus explains, *ut refrigeraret tam ferventem animum, incendere corpus deliberat* ("to cool her fervent soul, she thought to burn her body") (Fortunatus, "De vita S. Radegundis," 26:373). See also McNamara et al., eds., *Sainted Women of the Dark Ages* (Durham, NC: Duke University Press, 1992), 81.

5. Rom 8:28.

6. The place "where water should come from" is the urethral meatus, suggesting that Christina attacks her sexual organs. More specifically, one might think of the clitoris, which is anatomically close to the urethral meatus. The description of introducing material "into the body," however, means that we deal with an orifice, most likely the vagina, as the target of her self-inflicted punishment. For a discussion, see the Introduction, xvi–xvii; and Kirakosian, "Penitential Punishment and Purgatory."

7. See Ps 9:10.

8. See Lk 1:48.

CHAPTER 11

1. *Contra accidiam* is the title of this chapter and means "against sloth."

CHAPTER 12

1. *Contra jram* (spelling in the original) is the title of this chapter and means "against wrath."

2. The maneuver of biting her tongue may be understood as a type of spiritual circumcision. Examples of circumcision and castration of the tongue are discussed by medieval theologians; for a discussion of this, see Kirakosian, *Die Vita der Christina von Hane*, 147–150.

CHAPTER 13

1. *Contra superbiam* is the title of this chapter and means "against pride."

2. Although the concept of "public" is not the same in the Middle Ages, I have decided to translate the phrase *sie gynge da myt yn den chore vnder die lude* (*Vita*, 294) as "she walked into the choir publicly" because our modern understanding of "public" conveys the meaning of "being visible by others" best.

CHAPTER 14

1. *Contra gulam* is the title of this chapter and means "against gluttony."

CHAPTER 15

1. *Contra odium* is the title of this chapter and means "against hatred."

2. See Mt 5:44.

3. The reference to *grauffen broyt* in the original is unlikely to mean "gray bread," i.e. bread with no wheat, which was developed only in the early modern period. Taking the consonant variance of *ff* and *w* in late medieval Hessian dialects into account, *grauffe broyt* (normalized: *grawe brot*) can only mean "moldy bread." For further discussion and information on the dialect, see Kirakosian, *Die Vita der Christina von Hane*, 268–273.

4. The figure of drinking milk during infancy and then passing on to harsher treatment (in particular the whip) appears in Alan of Lille's *Anticlaudianus* (2.394–403). The use of whip and milk can also be found in Godfrey of St. Victor; see Godefridus de Sancto Victore, *Fons philosophiae*, 2.131–32: *Quorum potu lacteo reficit hiatus, / Virga quoque faciles corrigit erratus.*

CHAPTER 16

1. See 1 Thes 6:15; Rev 17:14.

2. It is unclear whether the sentence addressing Christ is spoken from Christina's perspective and thus part of her reflection and contemplation, or whether this is the narrator's voice addressing Christ (or perhaps even Christina?) in a prayerlike manner.

3. The qualification of the divinity and its gifts as being sweet (*soißicheit*) points to a sense-based acquisition of knowledge which has less to do with pleasure or actual taste than with the positive effects achieved through sensory perception. The etymology between *sapor* ("taste") and *sapientia* ("knowledge," "wisdom") justifies this connection. Mary Carruthers has shown that medieval Latin and vernacular writers employed "sweetness" to refer "to a definable sensory phenomenon"; see Carruthers, "Sweetness," 999.

CHAPTER 17

1. A chapel dedicated to Saint Nicholas cannot be found in any of the sources related to the convent of Hane; see Kirakosian, *Die Vita der Christina von Hane,* 131. The convent acquired a chapel in 1160, but no further details are known; see Kleinjung, "Die Herren von Bolanden," 29. The chapel to Saint Nicholas is also mentioned in Chs. 28 and 36 of the *Life.*

2. See Lk 22:44.

3. The Latin word *canticis* (with preposition *yn*) in the original refers to the Vulgata name ("Canticum Canticorum") of the book of the Bible, the Song of Songs.

4. See Sg 5:8.

CHAPTER 18

1. The theme of wounding Love, especially in conjunction with arrows that are "shot," can be found in religious texts as well as courtly love poetry, which is why I have decided to capitalize Love to mark its conceptual character in this instance. For this motif, see Newman, "'Love's Arrows.'"

2. The word *kußheit* (*Vita,* 298), here translated as "continence," may encompass more than just the concept of chastity (as it clearly does in Ch. 10) and refer generally to "modesty" and "abstinence."

CHAPTER 19

1. The monastic none (ninth hour) corresponds to 3 PM.

CHAPTER 20

1. If we are in 1288 (as the sequence of feast days and the later mention of 1288 suggest), Easter would fall on March 28.

2. It seems somewhat peculiar that Christina needs divine revelation to know what year it is. Perhaps this is to mark the degree to which she is removed from reality, as if she has lost track of time.

CHAPTER 21

1. Pentecost is celebrated on the seventh Sunday after Easter. In 1288 the evening before Pentecost was May 15.

2. The original Latin reads *O sapiencia Jhesu Christi* and evokes "wisdom" personified in Christ. It might be inspired by the first of the great antiphons of Advent in which seven titles are attributed to Jesus, the first one (sung on December 17) being that of Wisdom (Sapientia).

3. The original is ambiguous; it is also possible to translate as "The light embraced her."

4. The sentence beginning "I am all the abundant sweetness" is hard to understand and either fragmentary or erroneous in the original, where it reads: *Jch byn eyn genongede vnd dyne vbersoißicheit vnd aller begerlicher hertzen vnd aller heilger* (*Vita*, 300).

5. The two sentences beginning "The virtue of love" and "Mighty Love took the lead" are linked in the original. Without interpretation the original phrases are incomprehensible, as the grammatical structure is puzzling: *Vnd auch myt der dogent der lyebden, die myt yre also geweldenclichen ranck vnd yren lyeben an sich jn der selen czwanck, so name die krefftige lyebde vberthant, das der lyffe ynwendich zoreyße, daz sy den gebresten lyden moiste na godes willen vnd das auch gerne leyt* (*Vita*, 300).

CHAPTER 22

1. Corpus Christi is celebrated on the Thursday after Trinity Sunday, which is the first Sunday after Pentecost; in 1288 this would have been May 27.

2. The original wording *myt groißer genaden* (*Vita*, 301) is translated as "with great affection" rather than "with great mercy" because *genaden*—which can mean "favor," "grace," "mercy," "benevolence," "kindness," and "affection"—here refers to Christina's desire and not to a divine quality or action.

3. Christina is probably still in the infirmary, which explains why the priest transports the Eucharist outside the church. Christina follows his movements as she can here see beyond her room and through walls.

4. The concept of *fruitio*, enjoyment of the soul, is given here in the vernacular *gebruchen*, which is also attested for Hadewijch, Mechthild of Magdeburg, and Meister Eckhart; see Kirakosian, "Which Is the Greatest." In this instance we can sense that the compilers of the *Life* had thorough knowledge of vernacular mystical theology.

5. The sensation Christina experiences is placed in a particular moment: between the reception and the transformation of the Eucharist in her own body and soul. The detailed ensuing vision lays out how in that particular moment the soul is prepared for the transformation of Christ in her. Eucharistic visions connected to consumption and bodily senses are similarly vivid for Hadewijch; for a discussion of Hadewijch's Eucharistic visions, see Rudy, *Mystical Language of Sensation*, esp. 69: ". . . she [Hadewijch] insists that by imitating Christ (as by ingesting the bread of the Eucharist) we know and achieve unity with God as whole persons and with the help of our bodily senses."

6. The concept of *clairheit* (*Vita*, 338), here translated as "clarity," allows for multiple understandings, including brightness, lucidity, and brilliance. Re "heart": it is not clear whose heart is meant with "our heart"; perhaps a general "all of our hearts"?

7. See Ez 17:3–7.

8. *Ego sum panis vivus* ("I am the living bread") is the antiphon to the Benedictus of lauds on the feast of Corpus Christi. The antiphon is the piece of music that surrounds the Benedictus, which is the canticle for the office of lauds, one of the major offices sung at dawn. The original response is *Si quis manducaverit ex hoc pane, vivet in æternum* (stemming from the Vulgate Jn 6:25, meaning "Whoever eats from this bread will have eternal life"); but in Christina's vision the "dawn chorus" of birds changes the wording in order to sing to Jesus, their words, *Tu es panis vivus, in quo omnes vivimus in eternum* ("You are the living bread in which all of us have eternal life"), confirming their status as saved souls.

9. The last phrase, "which I cannot all tell," could be either posited from Christina's perspective or that of the narrator. The original text is ambiguous, although in my edition from 2017 I have opted to place the speech marks so that the words are Christina's (Kirakosian, *Die Vita der Christina von Hane*, 301).

CHAPTER 23

1. The Feast of Saint John the Baptist is celebrated on his Nativity, that is, on June 24.

2. The word for *curia* in the original is *houe,* meaning literally "court," and here specifically "papal court."

3. What is here translated as a faculty of the soul (intellect) stands for the part of the soul that is able to gain insight. The corresponding word, literally meaning "understanding," in the original is *verstentenyß* (*Vita,* 302).

4. The described battle is that of Worringen on June 5, 1288. The bishop's banner was carried by Count Adolf of Nassau, who was later to become king of Germany. The counts of Nassau were related to the counts of Bolanden, who had founded the convent of Hane. All this indicates that Christina may have been a sister of Adolf of Nassau. For a discussion of the historical correlations, see Mittermaier, "Wo lebte die selige Christina."

CHAPTER 24

1. The original word *wyne* (*Vita,* 302) for "beloved" is archaic in comparison to the rest of the text, and refers to the mystical lover.

2. This final passage containing the words of a visionary tune is highly poetic and marked by internal rhymes (*Vita,* 303).

CHAPTER 25

1. "To die a terrible death" (*eyns boißen doitze . . . sterben*), in line with medieval German texts, means that the man is to die unnaturally and in connection with a crime.

2. The word *frauwe* (*Vita,* 303), here translated as "magistra," literally means a woman of noble descent or mistress (in the sense of a ruler) and would most likely be the convent's leader (prioress), who is called "magistra" in the Premonstratensian Order.

CHAPTER 26

1. Re "sister-in-law": if Christina was indeed a sister of Adolf of Nassau, one of her sisters-in-law (married to Adolf) could have been Imagina von Isenburg-Limburg, who is known to have had three brothers; on the history of the family of Limburg, see Nieder, *Die Limburger Dynasten.* Lahnstein is a city in the Rhineland-Palatinate located at the confluence of the river Lahn with the Rhine.

2. The early death of two children of Adolf of Nassau was widely

known in the centuries that followed Christina's life; see Mittermaier, "Wo lebte die selige Christina," 88–89n82.

CHAPTER 27

1. The apparition of Mary visualizes the words of the sequence *Ave praeclara maris stella*, a memorial chant sung on Mary's Assumption. A concrete moment within the liturgical chant is marked: at the seventh verse, which starts with the words *Audi nos*, Christina observes Mary doing what the convent had previously prayed for in the fifth verse: *Ora, virgo, nos illo pane caeli dignos effici*; see Herimannus Contractus, "In assumptione B. Mariae," 241:313–314.

2. Christina imitates the kneeling Mary when she hears the bell rung for the evening prayer, calling on her to pray the *Ave Maria* (the Angelic Salutation, also *angelus*). The *angelus* in particular, introduced in the mid-thirteenth century by Franciscans, had found quick dissemination and papal confirmation; see Crăciun, "'Ora pro nobis,'" 109. It is unclear whether the convent of Hane in Christina's lifetime already possessed a specific *angelus* bell for this purpose. In any case, the sound of the bell incites Christina to perform a Hail Mary. Moreover, her prayer is an opportunity to practice *imitatio Mariae*, since Christina's devotional act becomes a reenactment of the preceding Marian vision triggered by the monastic soundscape.

CHAPTER 28

1. The original specifies a *bylde vnser lyeber frauwen*, but during Christina's lifetime this would have been a sculpture (in contrast to a portrait). For a discussion of the animated sacred object representing a vindictive Mary in its historical and legendary context, see Kirakosian, "La vision spirituelle."

CHAPTER 29

1. The feast day of Mary's Assumption is celebrated on August 15. The designation *assumpcionis beate et gloriose virginis Marie* (spelling in the original) means the "assumption of the blessed and mighty virgin Mary."

2. The seven precepts, instructions, or literally "wisdoms" taught to Christina correlate to the Solomonic Throne (see 1 Kgs 10:8–9), which in medieval exegesis comes to stand for the Marian Throne as the *sedes sapentiae* (see Rubin, *Mother of God*, 142). This analogy between Christina and the Virgin Mary is the first of a series of instances in which the mystic takes on Marian qualities. For a discussion of the seven precepts taught to Christina

in terms of asceticism and historical Marian devotion, see Kirakosian, *Die Vita der Christina von Hane*, 201–202.

CHAPTER 30

1. The Nativity of the Virgin Mary is celebrated on September 8.

2. *Canticis canticorum* (spelling in the original) is the Latin title for the Old Testament Song of Songs (see also Ch. 17, n. 3).

3. See Sg 7:8.

4. The word *breyt* (*Vita*, 305) is here translated as "all-encompassing," but it literally means "broad" or "wide."

5. The formulation *ich hayn dich verbreytde yn der lyebden* (*Vita*, 306) is here translated as "I have reinforced you in love," but it literally means "I have made you wider in love." The vision's imagery of a wide treetop is linguistically reflected in the discursive part as well as direct speech in this chapter by the repetition of *breyt/verbreytde*. For a discussion of the vision, see Kirakosian, *Die Vita der Christina von Hane*, 181–182.

CHAPTER 31

1. Archangel Michael is celebrated on September 29.

2. See Rev 22:13.

3. See Jn 8:12.

4. What I render here as "it" is in the original German "she," which means that it can refer to either the soul (feminine in German) or Christina. As referring to her soul, the sentence would be spoken from Christina's perspective, as indicated in the translation. An alternative interpretation would be to end the direct speech with the previous sentence, so that the chapter's final sentence would be narrative and referring to either Christina or her soul being unified with God; both "she was unified . . ." and "her soul was unified . . ." would then be possible interpretations.

CHAPTER 32

1. The feast day of Saint Ursula (also of the Eleven Thousand Virgins), celebrated on October 21, refers to an early martyr who according to medieval legend was killed alongside eleven thousand virgins. The legend has different versions and was particularly popular in and around Cologne. See Montgomery, *Saint Ursula and the Eleven Thousand Virgins*.

2. Martyrs' relics are nowhere else attested for the convent of Hane, but there is a connection between the legend of the Eleven Thousand Virgins

and the Premonstratensian Order: Hermann Joseph of Steinfeld was probably the author of a hymn in honor of Saint Ursula and her companions; see Hermannus Iosephus, "O vernantes Christi Rosae."

3. Elsewhere I have suggested that *spielle* (*Vita*, 308), here "pastime," be translated as "game," since in other bridal mystical texts Middle High German *spil* means Latin *connubium* ("marriage" or "marital intercourse"), forming part of a mystical language of desire; see Kirakosian, "Musical Heaven and Heavenly Music," 128–130.

4. For a discussion of the round dance and the correlation of vision and music, see Kirakosian, "Musical Heaven and Heavenly Music."

CHAPTER 33

1. All Saints Day is celebrated on November 1.

2. The original has three different words in a row to denote the convent's church: *gotz huße, kyrche, munster* (*Vita*, 308).

3. Christina's vision of a bleeding host strongly evokes host miracles as they have been reported for Germany between 1300 and 1550; see Bynum, "Bleeding Hosts."

CHAPTER 35

1. Epiphany is celebrated on January 6.

2. According to the medieval calendar Epiphany still belongs to the previous year, hence the indication 1289.

3. The phrase *Vnd vber dyß sal ich dyr geben eyn vber fludige maiße* (*Vita*, 309) is translated here as "Moreover, I shall give you these in overflowing measure," meaning that the measure is not a fourth additional gift but the abundance with which the three are given. Literally, however, the "overflowing measure" or "overflowing nature" is added to the three former gifts as a separate one.

CHAPTER 36

1. The liturgical feast day *Purificatio Mariae* (in the original *purificacionis*), also called Candlemas, falls on February 2 (forty days after Christmas) and celebrates the Presentation of Jesus in the Temple (Lk 2:22–40).

CHAPTER 37

1. The Annunciation of Mary is celebrated on March 25.

CHAPTER 38

1. The ten principles of wisdom revealed to Christina continue the instructive theme as first explored in Ch. 29 (see Ch. 29, n. 2).

2. See Mt 25:14–30 and Lk 19:11–28.

CHAPTER 39

1. See Jn 19:26.

2. See Jn 13:23.

3. The phrase *die also vnsprechlichen vnuerstendich synt vnser groppicheit zo begryffen, als eynem wayllen eynen dutzen zo verstayn* (*Vita*, 313) most likely means "which are as inexpressibly incomprehensible to our rough minds as German is to a foreigner." Literally, a Romance-speaking person is contrasted with a German-speaking one: "as if a foreigner was asked to understand a German." The form *wayllen* corresponds to Middle Low German *wāle/walen*. Elsewhere I argued that *dutzen* may be understood as a "poke" and *wayllen* as a "whale," which would then hint at a reception of the legends of Saint Brendan; for a discussion, see Kirakosian, *Die Vita der Christina von Hane*, 77, 125–126.

CHAPTER 40

1. The original gives a Latinate feast day: *Jn dem hogetzijt Agnetis virginis.* Saint Agnes is celebrated on January 21.

CHAPTER 41

1. *Purificatio Mariae* is celebrated on February 2.

CHAPTER 42

1. Invocavit Sunday or Quadragesima Sunday is the Sunday after Ash Wednesday.

2. See Sg 8:6.

CHAPTER 43

1. Maundy Thursday in the original is called "the supper of the Lord" (*abent eßen des heren*).

CHAPTER 45

1. The Feast of Saint John Before the Latin Gate is celebrated on May 6.

CHAPTER 46

1. The Feast of the Ascension falls on the fortieth day after Easter, a Thursday.

CHAPTER 47

1. Pentecost is celebrated on the seventh Sunday after Easter.

CHAPTER 48

1. Corpus Christi is celebrated on the Thursday after Trinity Sunday, which is the first Sunday after Pentecost.

CHAPTER 49

1. The Nativity of the Saint John the Baptist is celebrated on June 24.

CHAPTER 50

1. Saint Ulric of Augsburg (c. 890–973) is celebrated on July 4.

CHAPTER 51

1. Saint Mary Magdalene is celebrated on July 22.

2. Who exactly is meant with Hertwig is unclear. Most likely she was a canoness at Hane who had passed away during Christina's lifetime.

CHAPTER 52

1. The feast day of Mary's Assumption is celebrated on August 15.

2. See Sg 5:8.

3. The Beheading of Saint John the Baptist is commemorated on August 29.

4. See Prv 13:24.

CHAPTER 53

1. The Nativity of the Virgin Mary is celebrated on September 8.

2. See Sg 4:16. For a discussion of the metaphor of the garden as the place of delight, see Kirakosian, *Die Vita der Christina von Hane*, 171, 184–193.

CHAPTER 54

1. Archangel Michael is celebrated on September 29.

CHAPTER 55

1. The feast day of Saint Ursula, also of the Eleven Thousand Virgins, is celebrated on October 21.

CHAPTER 56

1. All Saints is celebrated on November 1. However, as later becomes evident, the recounted vision refers to the eve of All Saints, that is to October 31.

2. This is the first of a series of the same rhetorical question addressed to Christina, here in the form of *wes begerstu nu me* (*Vita,* 316). It also appears as *was wyltu me.*

3. See Sg 8:2.

4. See Mt 25:34.

5. The whole section starting "Afterward she saw" until the end of the chapter could be spoken from Christina's perspective; the pronoun "she" would then refer to her soul.

6. The intellect (in the oirignal: *vernoifft*) is a faculty of the soul according to medieval philosophy.

7. For a discussion of the concept of love-drunkenness, which is connected to the exegetic tradition of Sg 5:1, see Kirakosian, *Die Vita der Christina von Hane,* 188–189.

CHAPTER 57

1. The concept of the inner human being stands in an Eckhartian tradition and is linked to the nobility of the soul; for a discussion of Eckhart's understanding of the inner human, see Mieth, "The Outer and Inner Constitution," 71–78.

CHAPTER 58

1. Saint Catherine of Alexandria is celebrated on November 25.

2. The three instances of direct address in this paragraph are all in the second person plural in the original.

CHAPTER 59

1. The Presentation of the Blessed Virgin Mary is celebrated on November 21.

2. The word for "stream" is *ynfloiße* in the original (*Vita,* 319), which to-

gether with the movement of infusion and effusion evokes the Neoplatonic notion of emanation.

3. The phrase *Du salt got durch got laißen* (*Vita*, 319) could be literally translated as "You shall let go of God through God."

4. The entire sentence strongly suggests a reception of Meister Eckhart's thoughts on detachment (see discussion in the Introduction, xxvi–xxvii). Eckhart mentions detachment in connection with divine reward in one of his German sermons: *Der mensche, der alsô stât in gotes minne, der sol sîn selbes tôt sîn und allen geschaffenen dingen, daz er sîn selbes als wênic ahtende sî als eines über tûsent mîle. Der mensche blîbet in der glîcheit und blîbet in der einicheit und blîbet gar glîch; in in envellet kein unglîcheit. Dirre mensche muoz sich selben gelâzen hân und alle dise werlt. Wære ein mensche, des alliu disiu werlt wære, und er sie lieze als blôz durch got, als er sie enpfienc, dem wölte unser herre wider geben alle dise werlt und ouch daz êwige leben* (Meister Eckhart, "Predigt Q 12," in Meister Eckhart, *Die deutschen und lateinischen Werke: Die deutschen Werke*, vol. 1: *Meister Eckharts Predigten [1–24]*, ed. Josef Quint [Stuttgart: W. Kohlhammer, 1958, repr. 1986], 201–202). Translation in Meister Eckhart, "Sermon 57," in *The Complete Mystical Works of Meister Eckhart*, trans. Maurice O'C. Walshe (New York: Crossroad, 2009), 298: "That man who is established thus in God's love must be dead to self and all created things, paying as little regard to himself as to one who is a thousand miles away. That man abides in likeness and abides in unity in full equality, and no unlikeness enters into him. This man must have abandoned self and all this world. If there were a man who possessed all the world, and if he gave it up barely, just as he received it, for God's sake, then our Lord would give him back all this world and eternal life as well."

CHAPTER 60

1. Saint Nicholas is celebrated on December 6.

CHAPTER 61

1. The self-annihilation expressed in this passage is reminiscent of Meister Eckhart's ideas on detachment.

CHAPTER 62

1. The Christmas mass is the midnight mass on Christmas Eve (December 24), suggesting that Ch. 61 also refers to Christmas Eve.

2. See Sg 2:14.

3. See Sg 5:6. The failing soul is literally described as a melting soul (*Myn sele ist weche geworden*), in accordance with the Bible text (*Anima mea liquefacta est*). For a discussion of the liquefaction of the soul in the German mystical tradition, see Kirakosian, *Die Vita der Christina von Hane*, 236–240.

CHAPTER 63

1. Childermas or Innocents' Day is observed on December 28.

2. Saint Agnes is celebrated on January 21.

3. The monastic hours sext until none correspond to 9 AM to 3 PM.

4. See Rev 12:1. For a discussion of the crowning motif also in regard to Marian imagery, see Kirakosian, *Die Vita der Christina von Hane*, 214–217.

5. It is unclear what *vollenhyrtunge* (*Vita*, 322), here translated as "persistence," means. I have opted to translate it as related to Latin *duratio*, which would suggest that Christina is told that her body would manage to cope with the inflicted ailments until the end of her life.

CHAPTER 64

1. *Purificatio Mariae* is celebrated on February 2.

2. Candlemas, in the original *lyecht mysse* (*Vita*, 322), is another term for *Purificatio Mariae*.

3. Although this sentence is more likely to be spoken by Christina than by the divine voice, nothing indicates a shift from one speaker to the other.

CHAPTER 65

1. It is unclear who is meant with "they"; perhaps the sisters in Christina's convent?

2. See Prv 17:3.

CHAPTER 66

1. Invocavit Sunday or Quadragesima Sunday is the Sunday after Ash Wednesday.

CHAPTER 67

1. For a discussion on the Seven Joys of Mary, see Kirakosian, *Die Vita der Christina von Hane*, 200–201.

2. The Annunciation of Mary is celebrated on March 25.

CHAPTER 68

1. Passion Sunday is the fifth Sunday of Lent, that is, one week before Palm Sunday and two weeks before Easter.

2. The sentence is fragmentary. The whole passage is repetitive and barely comprehensible, suggesting several copy mistakes.

3. *Dominica in passione* is the Latin term for the same feast day, Passion Sunday.

CHAPTER 69

1. The Latin phrase translates as "On Maundy Thursday he said once more to her soul."

2. The last two sentences are in second person plural, though it is not clear who else other than Christina could be addressed.

CHAPTER 70

1. The Resurrection of Christ is celebrated on Easter.

CHAPTER 71

1. The Feast of the Ascension falls on the fortieth day after Easter, a Thursday.

CHAPTER 72

1. Pentecost is celebrated on the seventh Sunday after Easter.

2. The motifs of the Book of Life and the Seven-Sealed Book are from the Revelation of John and traditionally figure as Christological metaphors. The abstract and the conceptual meet in these book metaphors: Christina becomes analogous both to Christ and to the material book of her *Life*, which is also referred to as a book (Ch. 6). The whole passage, especially in connection with the seven gifts of the Holy Spirit, is reminiscent of the vernacular *Legatus divinae pietatis*, where Christ uses the same metaphors to apply them to the material book containing Gertrude of Helfta's hagiography: *Das bůch wil ich decken mit minem heiligen leben . . . und wil es versygelen mit miner gŏtlichen krafft, mit den sůben goben des heiligen geistes reht also mit sůben ingesygelen* (Gertrud von Helfta, *Ein botte der gŏtlichen miltekeit*, 3:26–29). For further discussion of book motifs in *The Life of Christina of Hane*, see Kirakosian, *Die Vita der Christina von Hane*, 221–249.

CHAPTER 73

1. The Feast of Saint John the Baptist is celebrated on his Nativity, June 24.

CHAPTER 74

1. Saint Mary Magdalene is celebrated on July 22.

CHAPTER 75

1. The feast day of Mary's Assumption is celebrated on August 15.

CHAPTER 76

1. The Beheading of Saint John the Baptist is commemorated on August 29.

CHAPTER 77

1. All Saints is celebrated on November 1, so this is about October 31.

CHAPTER 78

1. The corresponding word for "intellect" in the original is *vberst verstentenyß* (literally, "highest understanding"); see also above, Ch. 23, n. 3; and Ch. 56, n. 5.

2. The corresponding expression for "unmediated" is *sonder alle hyndernyß* (literally, "without any obstacle"). The concept and wording, especially in conjunction with God's will, are reminiscent of the reception of Meister Eckhart's description of an unmediated union with God. The passage from *The Life of Christina of Hane* reverberates poignantly with one particular passage in the so-called *Liber Positionum*, a collection of sentences that partly quotes Eckhart directly, edited in Pfeiffer, *Deutsche Mystiker des vierzehnten Jahrhunderts*, 678n148. For a description of the *Liber Positionum* in the context of its reception history, see Gottschall, "Eckhart and the Vernacular Tradition."

CHAPTER 80

1. Epiphany is celebrated on January 6.

2. Translated as "fainting of the mind," the original reads *amechtiget jres hertzes* (*Vita*, 330–331), which literally refers to an "unconsciousness of her heart."

3. The wording in the original, *siche* (*Vita*, 331), could also be translated as "behold," but because an intertextual reference follows, what is probably meant is to "look up" a specific passage.

4. The passage referred to appears above as Chapter 57.

5. The shift to present tense occurs abruptly, between the account of frequent ecstasy and the acute desire for unification. In this way, Christina's voice is more immediate than that of the narrator when it comes to vivid expressions.

6. The scribe noted *menschelicher bescheytdenheit* (*Vita*, 331), which may be translated as "human modesty," "human discretion," or—as suggested in my translation—"human prudence."

7. It is unclear what is meant by *gegruntfft* (*Vita*, 332), here translated as "grounded"; it could possibly mean "shouted" or even "roared."

8. The cosmological dimension of Christina's soul stylizes her as heavenly queen, a role that is traditionally reserved to the Virgin Mary; see discussion in the Introduction, xxvii–xxviii.

9. The word *bloitende* (*Vita*, 332), here translated as "flowering," could also mean "bleeding." The homophony between the two etymologically distinct words is striking in the *Life*, as in a number of cases either meaning could apply. I have opted for "flowering, "blossoming," and "blooming" in such ambiguous cases because these translations are congruent with the images of roses, lilies, and other flowers mentioned in the *Life*.

10. The word *hemel* (*Vita*, 332), which I render as "firmament," is literally "sky" or "heaven".

CHAPTER 81

1. Saint Agnes is celebrated on January 21.

2. The original reads that the first stone "was" the remarkable joy, therefore not explicitly marking a representative relationship between the stone and the feeling of joy. I have chosen to translate the phrase *Der irste steyn, der yn der cronen was, das waz* (*Vita*, 333) as "The first stone contained in the crown symbolized." The same holds for the next phrases describing the other two stones.

3. The wedding band is a motif in bridal mysticism that marks the election and confirmation of the bride of God. The final line of this chapter, if evoking a bleeding rose (see below, n. 6), would connect the spiritual betrothal to Christina's physical ailment. A link between the ring motif and

illness is most poignantly outlined in the *Legatus divinae pietatis,* which deals with the life and revelations of Gertrude of Helfta: *sicut annulus signum est desponsationis, sic adversitas tam corporalis quam spiritualis verissimum signum est electionis divinae et quasi desponsatio animae cum Deo* (2.1, p. 18); translated by Barratt, *Gertrude the Great of Helfta,* 29: "just as a ring is a sign of betrothal, so misfortune, both physical and spiritual, is a most certain sign of divine election and is, so to speak, the soul's betrothal to God."

4. See 2 Chr 9:17.

5. See Sg 4:19.

6. In the original the word for "blooming" is *bloytende* (*Vita,* 333) and could again mean "bleeding"; see above, Ch. 80, n. 9.

CHAPTER 82

1. Saint Gregory is today celebrated on September 3, but during the Middle Ages he was celebrated on March 12, which certainly fits the chronology of the *Life* better, this chapter being situated between Saint Agnes (January 21) and Easter.

2. In the original passage, all pronouns are the third-person feminine "she," making it impossible to distinguish between Christina and her soul.

CHAPTER 83

1. It is not clear how the last phrase of the sentence fits into the overall structure, here translated as "they hold for each other," from the original *die sie entgene eyn ander haynt* (*Vita,* 334).

CHAPTER 84

1. The Feast of the Ascension falls on the fortieth day after Easter, a Thursday.

CHAPTER 85

1. Pentecost is celebrated on the seventh Sunday after Easter.

2. The address as "blessed queen" and "jewel of women and of all the saints" puts Christina in parallel with the Virgin Mary, which is potentially heretical. For a discussion of the human-divine relationship between the mystic and Mary, see the Introduction, xxvii–xxxi.

3. The original phrase for "that you shall never part from me again" is

dastu nummerme salt gescheytden werden (*Vita*, 335). There is no specification as to what the soul shall never be separated from. In the translation I have therefore added an object ("from me").

4. Once more, *genaden* can be translated as "affection."

CHAPTER 86

1. Saint Mary Magdalene is celebrated on July 22.

2. The original has only "Oh soul."

3. It is not clear what the original *eyne sicher fryheit des gemoides* (*Vita*, 335) means. I have decided to translate it as "a firm freedom from ambition," but it could equally mean "a confirmed lack of intention."

CHAPTER 87

1. The feast day of Mary's Assumption is celebrated on August 15.

CHAPTER 88

1. The Nativity of the Virgin Mary is celebrated on September 8.

2. See Jn 1:14.

CHAPTER 89

1. The Archangel Michael is celebrated on September 29.

CHAPTER 90

1. The feast day of Saint Ursula, also of the Eleven Thousand Virgins, is celebrated on October 21.

CHAPTER 91

1. All Saints Day is celebrated on November 1.

CHAPTER 92

1. The terminology for the "wondrous pact of special love" is a legal one in the original text: *myt dießer wonderlicher hantfest sonderlicher lyebden* (*Vita*, 338). While the Middle High German adjective *hantveste* refers to being captivated, the noun *hantveste* describes a documented legal state in form of a charter or letter, and may also mean a legally defined privilege. In

the *Life*, its use means that the special love that Christina is embraced in is documented or guaranteed.

CHAPTER 93

1. Epiphany is celebrated on January 6.

CHAPTER 94

1. *Purificatio Mariae* is celebrated on February 2.

2. The garden motif belongs to the trope of the so-called *locus amoenus*, the place of delight; see above, Ch. 53, n. 2.

CHAPTER 95

1. The Annunciation of Mary is celebrated on March 25.

2. See above, Ch. 23, n. 3.

3. The original *dyne hertze bloet* (*Vita,* 339), here translated as "your heart blossoms" (accepting that "bloet" is shortened from *bloetende*), could be translated as "your heart bleeds." I have opted for the first for linguistic reasons and because the image of the blossoming heart is consistently evoked in the *Life;* see also above, Ch. 80, n. 9; Ch. 81, n. 6; and note 6 below.

4. It is unclear how the last phrase of the sentence, *dyn meynunge . . . geordeneret yn allen dyngen myt vffenbairer wairheit* (*Vita,* 339), here translated as "I have ordered your intentions through revealed truth," functions. The Middle High German verb employed in this phrase, *ordinêren,* can mean to order, command, ordain, or consecrate. Another interpretation could therefore read: "I have sanctified your intentions as is truly revealed." The original text may also carry the connotation of God's world order, so that another possible translation could read: "I have placed your intentions within the order of the revealed truth."

5. The original phrasing, *Durch der dogent willen alles, was du wylt, daz dat auch myn wylle ist* (*Vita,* 339), does not specify the quality of virtue. The phrase literally reads, "On the grounds of virtue, anything you will is also my will." I have chosen to translate Virtue as a conceptual principle (hence capitalized) rather than to add a new meaning (for example, "Anything you wish is likewise my will, because you are virtuous").

6. The original—*Dyne hertze bloet myt voiler genaden vnd dyne dogent bloitent myt heilgem wercke* (*Vita,* 339)—is ambiguous, as the word for blossoming and bleeding is mostly written in the same way in the *Life.* The

sentence could also be translated as "Your heart bleeds with full mercy and your virtues bleed with holy works," or a combination such as "Your heart blossoms with full mercy and your virtues bleed with holy works." See also above, note 3.

7. The original *pyne* (*Vita*, 340), here translated as "Passion," literally means pain or torment. However, the context makes it clear that Christ refers to the pain suffered in his death—that is, the Passion.

CHAPTER 96

1. Epiphany is celebrated on January 6.

CHAPTER 97

1. The beginning of the chapter starting with "On Easter" could be spoken from Christina's perspective, in which case she would refer to herself as "his bride."

2. Re "being": the wording in the original, *Wanne daz soiße mytweßen gotz yn der selen ist* (*Vita*, 341), is reminiscent of a sermon by Meister Eckhart. Cf. the use of the word *mitewesen*—meaning co-being, fellow essence, or joined being—in Meister Eckhart, "Sermon 77," in *Die deutschen und lateinischen Werke: Die deutschen Werke* 3:342–344: *Ze dem vierden mâle meinet ez die blôzen lûterkeit götlîches wesens, daz blôz âne allez mitewesen ist. Wan güete und wîsheit und swaz man von gote sprechen mac, daz ist allez mitewesen gotes blôzen wesens; wan alliu mitewesen machent ein vremde von dem wesene. Und alsô meinet daz wort "ich" gotes lûterkeit des wesens, daz dâ ist in im selben blôz âne alliu mitewesen, diu vremde und verre machent. . . . Aber ich gedâhte eines ûf dem wege, daz der mensche sô gar abegescheiden solte sîn in sîner meinunge, daz er nieman noch niht meinen ensolte wan die gotheit in ir selben, noch sælicheit noch diz noch daz wan aleine got als got und die gotheit in ir selber; wan, swaz dû anders meinest, daz ist allez ein mitewesen der gotheit. Dar umbe scheit abe allez mitewesen der gotheit, und nim sie blôz in ir selber.*

3. The word translated here as "music" is *geluyt* (*Vita*, 342), meaning "sound," "noise," or "toll" (bells chiming).

4. The wording in the original for what is here translated as "the depth of your groundless godhead," *yn der duyfften dyner grondeloißer gotheit* (*Vita*, 342), evokes the notion of the abyss as it is known from Meister Eckhart. For a discussion of the parallels between the *Life* and Eckhart's ground of the soul, see Kirakosian, *Die Vita der Christina von Hane*, 232–233.

5. The subject of the phrase is unclear: does God work the five responses in one person, or is it the person who does so, enjoying the unification? The male pronoun "he" (*er*) could refer to both God (*got*) and person (*mensche*) (*Vita*, 343).

CHAPTER 98

1. The Feast of Saint John the Baptist is celebrated on his Nativity, June 24.

2. The scholastic debate on the supremacy of knowledge or love begins as early as the mid-thirteenth century. See Ripelin, *Compendium theologicae veritatis*, esp. 2:62, p. 84: *Summa bonitas volens communicare bonum suum aliis, fecit creaturam rationale, quae summum bonum intelligeret, intelligendo amaret, amando possideret, possidendo beata est;* translated by Palmer, "The German Prayers," 1:382n18: "The greatest good, wishing to communicate its good to others, created a rational creature which would understand the greatest good, would by understanding love it, by loving possess it, and by processing it be sanctified." The issue of knowledge and love continued to be debated by mystics in the following centuries; see discussion in the Introduction, xxv–xxvi.

3. The last phrase is ambiguous: *Dan synt alle dynge vollenkomen yn gode, wanne iß wyrckeit an hyndernyß* (*Vita*, 343). What could the personal pronoun "it" (*iß*) refer to? The eternal life, which would be grammatically sound, but not mentioned in the close context? The unmediated presence of God stands in an Eckhartian tradition; see above, Ch. 78, n. 2. Elsewhere I have translated the final sentence as "Then all things are fulfilled in God as he works without obstacle"; Kirakosian, "Which Is the Greatest," 21.

CHAPTER 99

1. Corpus Christi is celebrated on the Thursday after Trinity Sunday, which is the first Sunday after Pentecost.

2. This angelic salutation is based on Lk 1:35, but with a considerable amount of variation and addition.

3. The description of this "baptism" is reminiscent of Jn 1:32 and Lk 3:22. The *Life* may be fragmentary here, since of the aforementioned four baptisms only one is explicitly listed, while the descriptions suggest that other kinds of baptisms are actually included.

4. It is not clear who speaks the words *dastu nyt moges sprechen, wie vyl gebresten du da habest, du habes ye myner genade entphangen* (*Vita*, 344), here translated as "and so no matter how many flaws you may have, you could

not therefore claim to receive less mercy." Directed at a thou they could be meant to be spoken by God.

CHAPTER 100

1. The Annunciation of Mary is celebrated on March 25.

2. Instead of "my soul," the original has the pronoun "she," *sie* (*Vita*, 344), which could refer to either Christina or her soul.

3. The phrase *Sye sprechent, myt den engelen ist* (*Vita*, 344), here translated as "They say that he speaks through angels," is ambiguous and could also mean "They say that he speaks to the angels."

4. The original wording for what is here translated as "God's outpouring—*Gat vße floiße* (*Vita*, 344)—is unclear. This entire passage in the *Life* on God's effusion, or literally "outflow," including the very final part, is overall reminiscent of the Neoplatonic concepts *ebullitio* and *bullitio;* for a discussion on Eckhart's Trinitarian theology as rooted within these concepts, see Reynolds, "'Bullitio' and the God beyond God."

5. The original wording for what is here translated as "the Father and the Son remain with the Spirit in eternity"—*der vader vnd der sone hugent jren geist yn der ewicheit* (*Vita*, 344)—employs the conceptual verb *hugen,* which is derived from Middle High German *gehugnisse,* meaning remembrance, memory, and imagination. The word *gehugnisse* is used by Meister Eckhart in a number of sermons, for example in Sermon 104, *In his, quae patris mei sunt, oportet me esse,* in Meister Eckhart, *Die deutschen und lateinischen Werke: Die deutschen Werke,* vol. 4,1, pp. 565–610, esp. 574, 585, 592.

6. This is a direct quote from the Vulgate; see Lk 1:38. The King James Bible translates it as "be it unto me according to thy word."

7. This is a direct quote from the Vulgate; see Lk 1:28. The King James Bible translates it as "Hail, thou that art highly favoured."

8. This sentence is fragmentary in the original. The verbal clause is not fully formed, so the sentence's full meaning remains obscure.

9. According to medieval theology, Mary conceived Christ in her heart; see Sahlin, *Birgitta of Sweden,* 85–87.

10. The *Life* has traditionally been thought to be fragmentary. Shifting the focus away from intention and toward effect, the abrupt ending—"etc."—performs an open-endedness, which is indeed the topic of the final chapter, in which the dying of the soul in God is described as a fluid and continuous process. See also the Introduction, xxxi–xxxii; and Kirakosian, *Die Vita der Christina von Hane,* 229–249.

References

PRIMARY SOURCES

Manuscripts

Braunfels, Archives of Count von Oppersdorff Solms-Braunfels, Antiquitates monasterii Aldenburgensis.

New Haven, Beinecke, MS 404.

Strasbourg, Bibliothèque nationale et universitaire, Ms. 324.

Edited and Translated Primary Sources

Alan of Lille. "Anticlaudianus." In *Literary Works,* edited and translated by Winthrop Wetherbee, 219–517. Dumbarton Oaks Medieval Library 22. Cambridge, MA: Harvard University Press, 2013.

Augustine. "De Genesi ad litteram XII." In *Patrologia cursus completus, omnium ss. patrum, doctorum scriptorumque ecclesiasticorum sive Latinorum, sive Graecorum. Series Latina,* edited by Jacques-Paul Migne, 34:245–486. Paris: Garnier Frères, 1845.

Barratt, Alexandra, trans. *Gertrude the Great of Helfta: The Herald of God's Loving-Kindness: Book Three.* Cistercian Fathers Series 63. Kalamazoo, MI: Cistercian Publications, 1999.

Boethius. "De institutione musica." In *Boetii de institutione arithmetica, libri duo: De institutione musica, libri quinque,* edited by Gottfried Friedlein, 175–371. Leipzig: Teubner, 1867; reprint Frankfurt: Minerva, 1966.

Contractus, Herimannus. "In assumptione B. Mariae." In *Analecta hymnica*

Medii Aevi, edited by Clemens Blume and Guido M. Dreves, vol. 50, no. 241. Leipzig: O. R. Reisland, 1907.

Craywinckel, Ludolphus van. "Het leven vande salighe maghet Christina." In *Legende der levens ende gedenck-weerdige daden van de voornaemste Heylige . . . in de witte orden van den H. Norbertus,* 2:730–759. Antwerp: Gerard Wolsschat, 1665.

Fischer, Bonifatius, Robert Weber, and Roger Gryson, eds. *Biblia sacra: Iuxta Vulgatam versionem.* 5th ed. Stuttgart: Deutsche Bibelgesellschaft, 2007.

Fortunatus. "De vita S. Radegundis. Libri duo." In *Fredegarii et aliorum chronica. Vae Sanctorum,* edited by Bruno Krusch, 358–395. Monumenta Germaniae Historica: Scriptores rerum merovingicarum [MGH SS rer. Merov.] 2. Hannover: Hahn, 1888.

Gerald of Wales. "Gemma ecclesiastica, distinction." In *Giraldi Cambrensis opera,* edited by J. S. Brewer, 2:105–107. London: Longman, 1869.

Gertrud von Helfta. *Ein botte der götlichen miltekeit.* Edited by Otmar Wieland. Studien und Mitteilungen zur Geschichte des Benediktiner-Ordens und seiner Zweige, Ergänzungsband 22. Ottobeuren: Bayerische Benediktinerakademie, 1973.

———. *Legatus divinae pietatis, III.* In *Gertrude d'Helfta, Oeuvres spirituelles III,* edited by Pierre Doyère. Sources chrétiennes: Série des textes monastiques d'Occident 27. Paris: Éditions du Cerf, 1968.

Gisilher von Slatheim. "Sermo de Sanctis." In *Paradisus anime intelligentis (Paradis der fornunftigen sele): Aus der Oxforder Handschrift Cod. Laud. Misc. 479 nach E. Sievers Abschrift,* edited by Philipp Strauch, 90–92. Deutsche Texte des Mittelalters 30. Berlin: Weidmann, 1919; reprint Hildesheim: Weidmann, 1998.

Godefridus de Sancto Victore. *Fons philosophiae.* Edited by Pierre Michaud-Quantin. Analecta Mediaevalia Namurcensia 8. Namur: Editions Godenne, 1956.

Hermannus Iosephus. "O venantes Christi Rosae." *Analecta hymnica Medii Aevi,* edited by Clemens Blume and Guido M. Dreves, vol. 50, no. 369. Leipzig: O. R. Reisland, 1907.

Kirakosian, Racha, ed. *Die Vita der Christina von Hane: Untersuchung und Edition.* Hermaea 144. Berlin: De Gruyter, 2017.

King, Margot, trans. *The Life of Christina Mirabilis.* Peregrina Translation Series 2. Toronto: Peregrina, 1989.

Lauer, Caspar. "Vita beatae Christinae." In *Spiritus literarius Norbertinus a scabiosis Casimiri Oudini calumniis vindicatur seu sylloge viros ex ordine Praemonstratensi,* edited by Georg Lienhard, 597–602. Augsburg: Matthäus Rieger, 1771.

McNamara, Jo Ann, John E. Halborg, and E. Gordon Whatley, eds. and trans. *Sainted Women of the Dark Ages.* Durham, NC: Duke University Press, 1992.

Mechthild von Magdeburg. *Das fließende Licht der Gottheit: Nach der Einsiedler Handschrift in kritischem Vergleich mit der gesamten Überlieferung,* edited by Hans Neumann. Vol. 1, *Text,* edited by Gisela Vollmann-Profe. Münchener Texte und Untersuchungen zur deutschen Literatur des Mittelalters 100. Munich: Artemis, 1990.

Meister Eckhart. *The Complete Mystical Works of Meister Eckhart.* Translated by Maurice O'C. Walshe. New York: Crossroad, 2009.

———. *Die deutschen und lateinischen Werke: Die deutschen Werke.* Vol. 1, edited by Josef Quint. Stuttgart: W. Kohlhammer, 1958; reprint 1986.

———. *Die deutschen und lateinischen Werke: Die deutschen Werke.* Vol. 3, edited by Josef Quint. Stuttgart: Verlag W. Kohlhammer, 1976.

———. *Die deutschen und lateinischen Werke: Die deutschen Werke.* Vol. 4,1, edited by Georg Steer. Stuttgart: W. Kohlhammer, 2003.

———. *Die deutschen und lateinischen Werke: Die deutschen Werke.* Vol. 5, *Meister Eckharts Traktate,* edited by Josef Quint. Stuttgart: W. Kohlhammer, 1963; reprint 1987.

———. *Liber Positionum.* In *Deutsche Mystiker des vierzehnten Jahrhunderts.* Vol. 2, *Meister Eckhart,* edited by Franz Pfeiffer, 628–684. Leipzig: G. J. Göschen, 1857.

Mittermaier, Franz Paul, ed. "Lebensbeschreibung der sel. Christina, gen. von Retters." *Archiv für mittelrheinische Kirchengeschichte* 17 (1965): 226–251; 18 (1966): 203–238.

Neidhart. *Neidhart-Lieder: Texte und Melodien sämtlicher Handschriften und Drucke.* Vol. 1, edited by Ulrich Miller et al. Berlin: De Gruyter, 2007.

Pinius, Joannes, ed. "Commentarius Praevus: Christina virgo, cognomento Mirabilis, Trudonopoli in Belgio (S.)," III. In *Acta Sanctorum* [AASS], *Jul. V [July 24], Julii, ex Latinis & Græcis... Tomus V,* edited by Joannes Baptista Sollerius, Joannes Pinius, Guilielmus Cuperus, and Petrus Boschius, 641A—643A. Antwerp: Jacobus du Moulin, 1727.

Pseudo-Isidore. *Conversion Legend of Mary Magdalene.* In *Exploring Medieval Mary Madgalene,* http://digital-editing.fas.harvard.edu.

Ripelin, Hugh. *Compendium theologicae veritatis.* In *B. Alberti Magni, Ratis-*

bonensis episcopi, Ordinis Prædicatorum, opera omnia, edited by Auguste Borgnet, 34:1–306. Paris: Vivès, 1895.

Schneider-Lastin, Wolfram, ed. "Leben und Offenbarungen der Elsbeth von Oye: Textkritische Edition der Vita aus dem 'Ötenbacher Schwesternbuch.'" In *Kulturtopographie des deutschsprachigen Südwestens im späteren Mittelalter: Studien und Texte,* edited by Barbara Fleith and René Wetzel, 395–448. Kulturtopographie des alemannischen Raums 1. Berlin: De Gruyter, 2009.

Strauch, Philipp, ed. *Die Offenbarungen der Adelheid Langmann: Klosterfrau zu Engelthal.* Quellen und Forschungen zur Sprach- und Kulturgeschichte der Germanischen Völker 26. Strasbourg: K. J. Trübner, 1878.

Thomas de Cantimpré. "Vita Beatae Christina Mirabilis Virginis." In *Acta Sanctorum* [AASS], *Jul. V [July 24], Julii, ex Latinis & Græcis . . . Tomus V,* edited by Joannes Baptista Sollerius, Joannes Pinius, Guilielmus Cuperus, and Petrus Boschius, 650A—660C. Antwerp: Jacobus du Moulin, 1727.

SECONDARY LITERATURE

Backmund, Norbert. *Die mittelalterlichen Geschichtsschreiber des Prämonstratenserordens.* Bibliotheca Analectorum Praemonstratensium 10. Averbode: Praemonstratensia, 1972.

———. *Monasticon Praemonstratense: Id est historia circariarum et canoniarum candidi et canonici Ordinis Praemonstratensis.* Vol. 1. Berlin: De Gruyter, 1983.

Bynum, Caroline W. "Bleeding Hosts and Their Contact Relics in Late Medieval Northern Germany." *Medieval History Journal* 7 (2004): 227–241.

Carruthers, Mary. "Sweetness." *Speculum* 81 (2006): 999–1013.

Crăciun, Maria. "'Ora pro nobis sancta Dei genitrix': Prayers and Gestures in Late Medieval Transylvania." In *Ritual, Images, and Daily Life: The Medieval Perspective,* edited by Gerhard Jaritz, 107–138. Vienna: Lit, 2012.

Cré, Marleen. *Vernacular Mysticism in the Charterhouse: A Study of London, British Library, MS Additional 37790.* Turnhout: Brepols, 2006.

Donnelly, John Patrick, SJ. "New Religious Orders for Men." In *Reform and Expansion 1500–1600,* edited by Ronnie Po-chia Hsia, 162–179. The Cambridge History of Christianity 6. Cambridge: Cambridge University Press, 2007.

Ehlers-Kisseler, Ingrid. "Heiligenverehrung bei den Prämonstratensern: Die Seligen und Heiligen des Prämonstratenserordens im deutschen Sprachraum." *Rottenburger Jahrbuch für Kirchengeschichte* 22 (2003): 65–94.

Fleischer, Wolfgang. *Untersuchungen zur Palmbaumallegorie im Mittelalter.* Münchener Germanistische Beiträge 20. Munich: Fink, 1976.

Frings, Theodor. *Mittelfränkisch-niederfränkische Studien.* Vol. 1, *Das ripuarisch-niederfränkische Übergangsgebiet.* Beiträge zur Geschichte der deutschen Sprache und Literatur 41. Halle: Niemeyer, 1917.

Gilomen-Schenkle, Elsanne. "Double Monasteries in the South-Western Empire (1100–1230) and Their Women's Communities in Swiss Regions." In *Partners in Spirit: Women, Men, and Religious Life in Germany, 1100–1500,* edited by Fiona J. Griffiths and Julie Hotchin, 47–74. Medieval Women: Texts and Contexts 24. Turnhout: Brepols, 2014.

Gottschall, Dagmar. "Eckhart and the Vernacular Tradition: Pseudo-Eckhart and Eckhart Legends." In *A Companion to Meister Eckhart,* edited by Jeremiah Hackett, 509–551. Brill's Companions to the Christian Tradition 36. Leiden: Brill, 2013.

Griffiths, Fiona J., and Julie Hotchin. "Women and Men in the Medieval Religious Landscape." In *Partners in Spirit: Women, Men, and Religious Life in Germany, 1100–1500,* edited by Fiona J. Griffiths and Julie Hotchin, 1–45. Medieval Women: Texts and Contexts 24. Turnhout: Brepols, 2014.

Hamburger, Jeffrey F. *The Rothschild Canticles: Art and Mysticism in Flanders and the Rhineland circa 1300.* New Haven, CT: Yale University Press, 1990.

Hamburger, Jeffrey F., Eva Schlotheuber, Susan Marti, and Margot Fassler. *Liturgical Life and Latin Learning at Paradies bei Soest, 1300–1425: Inscription and Illumination in the Choir Books of a North German Dominican Convent.* 2 vols. Münster: Aschendorff, 2016.

Hasebrink, Burkhard. "'Mitewürker gotes': Zur Performativität der Umdeutung in den deutschen Schriften Meister Eckharts." In *Literarische und religiöse Kommunikation in Mittelalter und früher Neuzeit: DFG-Symposium 2006,* edited by Peter Strohschneider, 62–88. Berlin: De Gruyter, 2009.

Heim, Manfred. "Prämonstratenser." In *Mönchtum, Orden, Klöster: Von Den Anfängen bis ur Gegenwart: Ein Lexikon,* edited by Georg Schwaiger, 355–366. Munich: Beck, 1994.

Horst, Ulrich. *Die Diskussion um die Immaculata Conceptio im Dominikaner-orden: Ein Beitrag zur Geschichte der theologischen Methode.* Veröffent-lichungen des Grabmann-Institutes zur Erforschung der Mittelalter-lichen Theologie und Philosophie, n.F. 34. Paderborn: F. Schöningh, 1987.

Huck, Oliver. "The Music of the Angels in Fourteenth- and Early Fifteenth-Century Music." *Musica Disciplina* 53 (2003–2008): 99–119.

Ilnitschi, Gabriela. "'Musica mundana': Aristotelian Natural Philosophy, and Ptolemaic Astronomy." *Early Music History* 21 (2002): 37–74.

Izbicki, Thomas. *The Eucharist in Medieval Canon Law.* New York: Cam-bridge University Press, 2015.

———. "The Immaculate Conception and Ecclesiastical Politics from the Council of Basel to the Council of Trent: The Dominicans and Their Foes." *Archiv für Reformationsgeschichte* 96 (2005): 145–170.

Jackson, Timothy R. "Versehrtheit, Unversehrtheit und der auferstandene Körper." In *Verletzungen und Unversehrtheit in der deutschen Literatur des Mittelalters: XXIV Anglo-German Colloquium, Saarbrücken 2015,* edi-ted by Sarah Bowden, Nine Miedema, and Stephen Mossman, 141–154. Tübingen: Narr Dr. Gunter, 2020.

Kirakosian, Racha. "Das göttliche Herz im 'Fließenden Licht der Gottheit' Mechthilds von Magdeburg: Eine motivgeschichtliche Verortung." *Euphorion* 111 (2017): 257–275.

———. "Musical Heaven and Heavenly Music: At the Crossroads of Li-turgical Music and Mystical Texts." *Viator* 48 (2017): 121–144.

———. "Penitential Punishment and Purgatory: A Drama of Purification through Pain." In *Punishment and Penitential Practices in Medieval Ger-man Writing,* edited by Sarah Bowden and Annette Volfing, 129–153. King's College London Medieval Studies 26. London: Boydell & Brewer, 2018.

———. "Rhetorics of Sanctity: Christina of Hane in the Early Modern Period—with a Comparison to a Mary Magdalene Legend." *Oxford German Studies* 43, no. 4 (December 2014): 380–399.

———. "La vision spirituelle dans l'espace corporel et le pouvoir performa-tif du langage dans la biographie mystique de Christina de Hane." *Le Moyen Âge* 123 (2017): 589–607.

———. *Die Vita der Christina von Hane: Untersuchung und Edition.* Her-maea 144. Berlin: De Gruyter, 2017.

———. "Which Is the Greatest—Knowledge, Love, or Enjoyment of

God? A Comparison between Christina of Hane and Meister Eckhart." *Medieval Mystical Theology* 23 (2014): 20–33.

Klapp, Sabine. "Negotiating Autonomy: Canons in Late Medieval 'Frauenstifte.'" In *Partners in Spirit: Women, Men, and Religious Life in Germany, 1100–1500*, edited by Fiona J. Griffiths and Julie Hotchin, 367–400. Medieval Women: Texts and Contexts 24. Turnhout: Brepols, 2014.

Kleinjung, Christine. "Die Herren von Bolanden als Klostergründer." *Alzeyer Geschichtsblätter* 33 (2001): 17–33.

Koch, Karl, and Eduard Hegel. *Die Vita des Prämonstratensers Hermann Joseph von Steinfeld: Ein Beitrag zur Hagiographie und zur Frömmigkeitsgeschichte des Hochmittelalters.* Colonia sacra 3. Cologne: Balduin Pick, 1958.

Köster, Kurt. "Christina von Hane (Hagen), gen. Retters." In *Die deutsche Literatur des Mittelalters: Verfasserlexikon: Begründet von Wolfgang Stammler, fortgeführt von Karl Langosch*, 2nd ed., edited by Kurt Ruh et al., 1:1225–1228. Berlin: De Gruyter, 1978.

———. "Leben und Gesichte der Christina von Retters (1269 bis 1291)." *Archiv für mittelrheinische Kirchengeschichte* 8 (1956): 241–269.

Krings, Bruno. "Die Frauenklöster in der Pfalz." *Jahrbuch für westdeutsche Landesgeschichte* 35 (2009): 113–202.

Kugler, Hermann Josef. *Hermann Josef von Steinfeld (um 1160–1241) im Kontext christlicher Mystik.* St. Ottilien: EOS, 1992.

Lamy, Marielle. *L'immaculée conception: Étapes et enjeux d'une controverse au Moyen-Âge, XIIe–XVe siècles.* Collection des études augustiniennes: Série Moyen-Âge et temps modernes 35. Paris: Institut d'études augustiniennes, 2000.

Largier, Niklaus. "Medieval Mysticism." In *The Handbook of Religion and Emotion*, edited by John Corrigan, 364–379. Oxford: Oxford University Press, 2008.

Leinsle, Ulrich G. "Zur rechtlichen Ordnung prämonstratensischer Seelsorge im Mittelalter." *Rottenburger Jahrbuch für Kirchengeschichte* 22 (2003): 31–46.

Martin, Roland. *Untersuchungen zur rhein-moselfränkischen Dialektgrenze.* Deutsche Dialektgeographie 11a. Marburg: N. G. Elwert, 1922.

McGinn, Bernard. *The Flowering of Mysticism: Men and Women in the New Mysticism, 1200–1350.* The Presence of God: A History of Western Christian Mysticism 3. New York: Crossroad Herder, 1998.

————. *The Foundations of Mysticism*. The Presence of God: A History of Western Christian Mysticism 1. New York: Crossroad, 1991.

————. "Meister Eckhart and the Beguines in the Context of Vernacular Theology." In *Meister Eckhart and the Beguine Mystics: Hadewijch of Brabant, Mechthild of Magdeburg, and Margerite Porete*, edited by Bernard McGinn, 1–14. New York: Continuum, 1994.

Mieth, Dietmar. "The Outer and Inner Constitution of Human Dignity in Meister Eckhart." In *Dynamics of Difference: Christianity and Alterity, a Festschrift for Werner G. Jeanrond*, edited by Ulrich Schmiedel and James M. Matarazzo, 71–78. London: Bloomsbury T&T Clark, 2015.

Mittermaier, Franz Paul. "Ein bislang verschollener Hymnus (v. Pieter de Waghenare) auf die sel. Christina, gen. von Retters." *Archiv für mittelrheinische Kirchengeschichte* 10 (1958): 353–355.

————. "Lebensbeschreibung der sel. Christina, gen. von Retters." *Archiv für mittelrheinische Kirchengeschichte* 17 (1965): 209–226.

————. "Das Verhältnis des Altenberger Priors Petrus Diederich (1643–1655) zu den Prämonstratenserstiften Ober- und Nieder-Ilbenstadt in der Wetterau." *Wetterauer Geschichtsblätter* 7/8 (1959): 117–131.

————. "Wo lebte die selige Christina, in Retters oder in Hane?" *Archiv für mittelrheinische Kirchengeschichte* 12 (1960): 75–97.

Montgomery, Scott B. *Saint Ursula and the Eleven Thousand Virgins of Cologne: Relics, Reliquaries, and the Visual Culture of Group Sanctity in Late Medieval Europe*. Oxford: Peter Lang, 2010.

Mossman, Stephen. "The Western Understanding of Islamic Theology in the Later Middle Ages: Mendicant Responses to Islam from Riccoldo da Monte di Croce to Marquard von Lindau." *Recherches de théologie et philosophie médiévales* 74 (2007): 169–224.

Muir, Carolyn Diskant. "Bride or Bridegroom? Masculine Identity in Mystic Marriages." In *Holiness and Masculinity in the Middle Ages*, edited by P. H. Cullum and Catherine J. Lewis, 58–78. Cardiff: University of Wales Press, 2004.

Newman, Barbara. "Book Review: Racha Kirakosian, *Die Vita der Christina von Hane: Untersuchung und Edition*." *Speculum* 94 (2019): 233–235.

————. "Contemplating the Trinity: Text, Image, and the Origins of the Rothschild Canticles." *Gesta* 52 (2013): 133–159.

————. *God and the Goddesses: Vision, Poetry, and Belief in the Middle Ages*. Philadelphia: University of Pennsylvania Press, 2003.

————. "'Love's Arrows': Christ as Cupid in Late Medieval Art and Devotion." In *The Mind's Eye: Art and Theological Argument in the Middle Ages*, edited by Jeffrey F. Hamburger and Anne-Marie Bouché, 263–286. Princeton, NJ: Princeton University, 2006.

Nieder, Franz-Karl. *Die Limburger Dynasten und die deutschen Könige 1292 bis 1356.* Nassauische Annalen 117. Wiesbaden: Verlag des Vereines für Nassauische Altertumskunde und Geschichtsforschung, 2006.

Palazzo, Eric. "Art, Liturgy, and the Five Senses in the Early Middle Ages." *Viator* 40 (2009): 25–56.

Palmer, Nigel F. "Das Buch als Bedeutungsträger bei Mechthild von Magdeburg." In *Bildhafte Rede in Mittelalter und früher Neuzeit: Probleme ihrer Legitimation und ihrer Funktion*, edited by Wolfgang Harms, 217–235. Tübingen: M. Niemeyer, 1992.

————. "The German Prayers in Their Literary and Historical Context." In Jeffrey F. Hamburger and Nigel F. Palmer, *The Prayer Book of Ursula Begerin*, 1:377–488. Dietikon-Zurich: Urs Graf Verlag, 2015.

————. "'In kaffin in got': Zur Rezeption des 'Paradisus anime intelligentis' in der Oxforder Handschrift MS. Laud. Misc. 479." In *"Paradisus anime intelligentis": Studien zu einer dominikanischen Predigtsammlung aus dem Umkreis Meister Eckharts*, edited by Burkhard Hasebrink, Nigel F. Palmer, and Hans-Jochen Schiewer, 69–131. Tübingen: Niemeyer, 2009.

Pies, Norbert J., and Werner P. Pfeil, eds. *Zur Geschichte von Kloster Maria Engelport*. 13 vols. Erftstadt: Pies & Pfeil, 1989–2000.

Rankins, Susan. "'Naturalis concordia vocum cum planetis': Conceptualizing the Harmony of the Spheres in the Early Middle Ages." In *Citation and Authority in Medieval and Renaissance Musical Culture: Learning from the Learned*, edited by Suzannah Clark and Elisabeth Eva Leach, 3–19. Studies in Medieval and Renaissance Music 4. Woodbridge, Suffolk: Boydell Press, 2005.

Rapp, Claudia. "Storytelling as Spiritual Communication in Early Greek Hagiography: The Use of Diegesis." *Journal of Early Christian Studies* 6 (1998): 431–448.

Reynaert, J. "Het vroegste middelnederlandse Palmboomtraktaat." *Ons geestelijk erf* 52 (1978): 296–310.

Reynolds, P.L. "'Bullitio' and the God beyond God: Meister Eckhart's Trinitarian Theology: Part II: Distinctionless Godhead and Trinitarian God." *New Blackfriars* 70, no. 827 (1989): 235–244.

Rubin, Miri. *Corpus Christi: The Eucharist in Late Medieval Culture.* Cambridge: Cambridge University Press, 1991.

———. *Mother of God: A History of the Virgin Mary.* New Haven, CT: Yale University Press, 2009.

Rudy, Gordon. *Mystical Language of Sensation in the Later Middle Ages.* Studies in Medieval History and Culture 14. New York: Routledge, 2002.

Ruh, Kurt. *Geschichte der abendländischen Mystik.* Vol. 2, *Frauenmystik und franziskanische Mystik der Frühneuzeit.* Munich: Beck, 1993.

Sahlin, Claire Lynn. *Birgitta of Sweden and the Voice of Prophecy.* Studies in Medieval Mysticism 3. Woodbridge, Suffolk: Boydell Press, 2001.

Sand, Alexa. "Vindictive Virgins: Animate Images and Theories of Art in Some Thirteenth-Century Miracle Stories." *Word & Image: A Journal of Verbal/Visual Enquiry* 26 (2010): 150–159.

Sansterre, Jean-Marie. "'Omnes qui coram hac imagine genua exerint . . .': La vénération d'images de saints et de la Vierge d'après les textes écrits en Angleterre du milieu du xie aux premières décennies du xiiie siècle." *Cahiers de civilisation médiévale* 49 (2006): 257–294.

Scheepsma, Wybren F. "Filling the Blanks: A Middle Dutch Dionysius Quotation and the Origins of the Rothschild Canticles." *Medium Ævum* 70 (2001): 278–303.

———. *The Limburg Sermons: Preaching in the Medieval Low Countries at the Turn of the Fourteenth Century.* Brill's Series in Church History 34. Leiden: Brill, 2008.

Schilp, Thomas. *Norm und Wirklichkeit religiöser Frauengemeinschaften im Frühmittelalter: Die Institutio sanctimonialium Aquisgranensis des Jahres 816 und die Problematik der Verfassung von Frauenkommunitäten.* Göttingen: Vandenhoeck & Ruprecht, 1998.

Schützeichel, Rudolf. *Mundart, Urkundensprache und Schriftsprache: Studien zur Sprachgeschichte am Mittelrhein.* Rheinisches Archiv 54. Bonn: Röhrscheid, 1960.

Stolz, Michael. "Maria und die Artes liberales: Aspekte einer mittelalterlichen Zuordnung." In *Maria in der Welt: Marienverehrung im Kontext der Sozialgeschichte 10.–18. Jahrhundert,* edited by Claudia Opitz et al., 95–120. Clio Lucernensis 2. Zurich: Chronos, 1993.

Uffmann, Heike. "Inside and Outside the Convent Walls: The Norm and Practice of Enclosure in the Reformed Nunneries of Late Medieval Germany." *Medieval History Journal* 4, no. 1 (2001): 83–108.

Valvekens, Emile. "Le chapitre général de Prémontré et les nouveaux statuts de 1505." *Analecta Praemonstratensia* 14 (1938): 53–94.

Warnar, Geert. "Men of Letters: Medieval Dutch Literature and Learning." In *University, Council, City: Intellectual Culture on the Rhine, 1300–1550: Acts of the XIIth International Colloquium of the Société Internationale pour l'Étude de la Philosophie Médiévale, Freiburg im Breisgau, 27–29 October 2004*, edited by Laurent Cesalli, Nadja Germann, and Maarten J. F. M. Hoenen, 221–246. Turnhout, Bel.: Brepols, 2007.

Watson, Nicholas. "Censorship and Cultural Change in Late-Medieval England: Vernacular Theology, the Oxford Translation Debate, and Arundel's Constitutions of 1409." *Speculum* 70 (1995): 822–864.

Webb, Heather. *The Medieval Heart*. New Haven, CT: Yale University Press, 2010.

Further Reading

PRIMARY SOURCES RELATED TO
CHRISTINA OF HANE

Craywinckel, Ludolphus van. "Het leven vande salighe maghet Christina." In *Legende der levens ende gedenck-weerdige daden van de voornaemste Heylige . . . in de witte orden van den H. Norbertus*, 2:730–759. Antwerp: Gerard Wolsschat, 1665.

Huybrechts, Frans. *Copperplate Engraving "Beata Christina a Christo."* Antwerp, 1662. In *Antiquitates monasterii Aldenburgensis*, Archives of Count Solms-Braunfels, Braunfels, 711.

Kirakosian, Racha, ed. "Die Vita der Christina von Hane." In *Die Vita der Christina von Hane: Untersuchung und Edition*, 283–349. Hermaea 144. Berlin: De Gruyter, 2017.

Lauer, Caspar: "Vita beatae Christinae." In *Spiritus literarius Norbertinus a scabiosis Casimiri Oudini calumniis vindicatur seu sylloge viros ex ordine Praemonstratensi*, edited by Georg Lienhard, 597–602. Augsburg: Matthäus Rieger, 1771.

Lienhard, Georg. *Spiritus Literarius Norbertinus . . . Ad Historiae Notitiam Facientibus Illustrata*, 351. Augsburg: Matthäus Rieger, 1771.

Mittermaier, Franz Paul, ed. "Lebensbeschreibung der sel. Christina, gen. von Retters." *Archiv für mittelrheinische Kirchengeschichte* 17 (1965): 226–251; 18 (1966): 203–238.

Spilbeeck, Ignace van. *Une fleur cachée: La bienheureuse Christine du Christ, religieuse du monastère de Rhetirs*. Namur: Douxfils, 1885.

Strasbourg, Bibliothèque nationale et universitaire, MS. 324

Waghenare, Pieter de. "Hymnus de B. Christina Monasterij Rhetersensis in Dioecesi Moguntina Ordinis Praemonstrat. Sanctimoniali." Appendix to *Vita beati Hermanni Josephi*, 2nd ed. Antwerp: Gerard Wolsschat, 1661 (first published without appendix, Cologne: Johann Busaeus, 1656).

STUDIES RELATED TO CHRISTINA OF HANE AND THE CONVENT OF HANE

Backmund, Norbert. *Die mittelalterlichen Geschichtsschreiber des Prämonstratenserordens*. Bibliotheca Analectorum Praemonstratensium 10. Averbode, Bel.: Praemonstratensia, 1972. (Diss., Munich.)

———. *Monasticon Praemonstratense: Id est historia circariarum et canoniarum candidi et canonici Ordinis Praemonstratensis*. Vol. 1. Berlin: De Gruyter, 1983.

Emmelius, Caroline. "Das visionäre Ich: Ich-Stimmen in der Viten- und Offenbarungsliteratur zwischen Selbstthematisierung und Heterologie." In *Von sich selbst erzählen: Historische Dimensionen des Ich-Erzählens: Tagung Irsee 2013*, edited by Sonja Glauch and Katharina Philipowski, 361–388. Studien zur historischen Poetik 26. Heidelberg: Universitätsverlag Winter, 2017.

Fink, Wilhelm. *Kloster (Hofgut) Retters v. d. Höh.* Königstein: [n.p.], 1931.

Frenken, Ralph. *Kindheit und Mystik im Mittelalter*. Beihefte zur Mediävistik 2. Frankfurt am Main: Peter Lang, 2002.

Górecka, Marzena. *Das Bild Mariens in der deutschen Mystik*. Deutsche Literatur von den Anfängen bis 1700 29. Bern: Peter Lang, 1999.

Jacob, Erwin. "Untersuchungen über Herkunft und Aufstieg des Reichsministerialengeschlechtes Bolanden." Diss., Giessen, 1936.

Kirakosian, Racha. "Musical Heaven and Heavenly Music: At the Crossroads of Liturgical Music and Mystical Texts." *Viator* 48 (2017): 121–144.

———. "Penitential Punishment and Purgatory: A Drama of Purification through Pain." In *Punishment and Penitential Practices in Medieval German Writing*, edited by Sarah Bowden and Annette Volfing, 129–153. Kings College London Medieval Studies 26. London: Boydell & Brewer, 2018.

———. "Rhetorics of Sanctity: Christina of Hane in the Early Modern Period—with a Comparison to a Mary Magdalene Legend." *Oxford German Studies* 43, no. 4 (December 2014): 380–399.

————. "La vision spirituelle dans l'espace corporel et le pouvoir performatif du langage dans la biographie mystique de Christina de Hane." *Le Moyen Âge* 123 (2017): 589–607.

————. *Die Vita der Christina von Hane: Untersuchung und Edition*. Berlin: De Gruyter, 2017.

————. "Which Is the Greatest—Knowledge, Love, or Enjoyment of God? A Comparison between Christina of Hane and Meister Eckhart," *Medieval Mystical Theology* 23 (2014): 20–33.

Kleinjung, Christine. "Die Herren von Bolanden als Klostergründer." *Alzeyer Geschichtsblätter* 33 (2001): 17–33.

Köster, Kurt. "Christina von Hane (Hagen), gen. Retters." In: *Die deutsche Literatur des Mittelalters: Verfasserlexikon: Begründet von Wolfgang Stammler, fortgeführt von Karl Langosch*, 2nd ed., edited by Kurt Ruh et al., 1:1225–1228. Berlin: De Gruyter, 1978.

————. "Leben und Gesichte der Christina von Retters (1269 bis 1291)." *Archiv für mittelrheinische Kirchengeschichte* 8 (1956): 241–269.

Krings, Bruno. "Die Frauenklöster in der Pfalz." *Jahrbuch für westdeutsche Landesgeschichte* 35 (2009): 113–202, at 172–202.

Mittermaier, Franz Paul. "Ein bislang verschollener Hymnus auf die sel. Christina gen. von Retters." *Archiv für mittelrheinische Kirchengeschichte* 10 (1958): 353–355.

————. "Lebensbeschreibung der sel. Christina, gen. von Retters." *Archiv für mittelrheinische Kirchengeschichte* 17 (1965): 209–251.

————. "Das Verhältnis des Altenberger Priors Petrus Diederich (1643/55) zu den Prämonstratenserstiften Ober- und Nieder-Ilbenstadt in der Wetterau." *Wetterauer Geschichtsblätter* 7/8 (1959): 117–131.

————. "Wo lebte die selige Christina, in Retters oder in Hane?," *Archiv für mittelrheinische Kirchengeschichte* 12 (1960): 75–97.

Murdoch, Brian. "Book Review: Racha Kirakosian, *Die Vita der Christina von Hane: Untersuchung und Edition*." *Medium Ævum* 87 (2018): 191–192.

Newman, Barbara. "Book Review: Racha Kirakosian, *Die Vita der Christina von Hane: Untersuchung und Edition*." *Speculum* 94 (2019): 233–235.

Obry, Karl. "Die Herren von Bolanden und ihr Hauskloster: 850 Jahre Kloster Hane (1129–1979)." *Donnersberg-Jahrbuch* 2 (1979): 102–108.

Peters, Wolfgang. "Springiersbacher Einflüsse in der Mainzer Erzdiözese: Zur Observanz des Kanonikerstiftes Bolanden in der ersten Hälfte des 12. Jahrhunders." *Archiv für mittelrheinische Kirchengeschichte* 30 (1978): 91–99.

Petit, François. *La spiritualité des Prémontrés aux XXe et XIIIe siècles.* Études de théologie de d'histoire de la spiritualité 10. Paris: J. Vrin, 1947.

Remling, Franz Xaver. *Urkundliche Geschichte der ehemaligen Abteien und Klöster im jetzigen Rheinbayern,* 151–164. Neustadt an der Haardt: Christmann, 1836.

Ruh, Kurt. *Geschichte der abendländischen Mystik.* Vol. 2, *Frauenmystik und franziskanische Mystik der Frühneuzeit,* 121–125. Munich: Beck, 1993.

Semmler, Josef. "Zu den Anfängen des Augustinerchorherrenstifts Bolanden." *Blätter für pfälzische Kirchengeschichte und religiöse Volkskunde* 24 (1957): 145–149.

Volfing, Annette. "Verdoppelung und Verdrängung: Simultane Diskurse in der mystischen Literatur." In *Stimme und Performanz in der mittelalterlichen Literatur,* edited by Nine Miedema, Angela Schrott, and Monika Unzeitig, 433–448. Historische Dialogforschung 4. Berlin: De Gruyter, 2017.

Weiss, Bardo. *Ekstase und Liebe: Die Unio mystica bei den deutschen Mystikerinnen des 12. und 13. Jahrhunderts.* Paderborn: Ferdinand Schöningh, 2000.

Index

Adolf of Nassau, xv, xlviinii, 106n4, 106ni (ch. 26), 106n2 (ch. 26)

Advent, xxvii, 84, 104n2 (ch. 21)

Agnes (saint's day), 60–61, 77, 110ni (ch. 40), 114n2 (ch. 63), 117ni, 118ni (ch. 82)

Alan of Lille, liin50, 102n4

All Saints Day, 39, 52–54, 59, 71–72, 74, 84, 109ni (ch. 33), 112ni (ch. 56), 116ni (ch. 77), 119ni (ch. 91)

Alsace, xv

Altenberg (convent), xxxiv, livn73; Gertrude of Altenberg, xxxiv

Angela von Foligno, xxi

Angels, xxvii, xxxvii, xlixn32, 2, 9, 12, 20, 24–25, 35, 37, 39, 43, 51, 55, 61, 64–65, 69, 71, 76–77, 80–83, 85–86, 91, 95–97; angelic spheres (choirs), xxviii, xlixn33, liin50, 52, 55, 60–62, 65, 73, 88, 95; Angels' song, xxiii, 25, 92; Archangel Gabriel, 39, 95–97; Archangel Michael, 36, 39, 52, 108ni (ch. 31), 111ni (ch. 54), 119ni (ch. 89)

Angelus bell, xvii, 33, 107n2 (ch. 27)

Antwerp, xxxvi–xxxvii, Fig. 3

Aquinas, Thomas, xxix–xxx

Ascension (of Christ), 49, 67, 111ni (ch. 46), 115ni (ch. 71), 118ni (ch. 84)

Asceticism, ix, xiii, xvi, 12–13, 16; of the Desert Fathers, xvi

Augustine, xxiv, xlixn36; Rule of Saint, xv

Ave Maria, 33, 107n2 (ch. 27)

Ave praeclara, 33, 107ni (ch. 27)

Bad Kreuznach, xxxvi

Beguines, xiii

Bernhard of Clairvaux, xiv, xxix

Boethius, xlixn32

Bolanden (place near Hane), xxxvii, 1; counts of Bolanden, xv, 106n4; Werner I of Bolanden (count), xv

Bollandists, xxxvii

Bonaventure, xxix

Brandan, lin49

Catherine of Alexandria (Saint's day), 57, 112ni (ch. 58)

Catherine of Siena, xxi, xxx

Childermas (Innocents' Day), 59, 114ni (ch. 63)

Christmas, xvii, 5, 40, 59, 74, 100n1
(ch. 5), 113n1 (ch. 62); Christmas
Eve, 5, 113n1 (Ch. 62)
Chronicles (books of the Bible),
lvin87, 188n4
Cologne, 30, 108n1 (ch. 32)
connubium, xiv, 109n3 (ch. 32)
Corpus Christi, xix, xlviin22, 28, 49,
94, 104n1 (ch. 22), 105n8, 111n1 (ch.
48), 122n1 (ch. 99)
Cosmos, xiii, xxiii, xxviii, xlixn32,
117n8
Council of Basel, xxx, liiin58
Counter-Reformation, xxxv, xxxix
Craywinckel, Ludolph van, xxxviii–
xxxix, lvn74, lvn76, lvn79, Fig. 4

David, King, 9
Diederich, Petrus, xxxiii, xxxvi–xl,
livn73
Dominica Invocavit (Quadragesima
Sunday), 47, 64, 110n1 (ch. 42),
114n1 (ch. 66)
Dominican Order, xiii, xvii, xxvi, xxx

Easter, xvii, xliv–xlv, 24, 44, 66, 79,
90–92, 104n1 (ch. 20)115n1 (ch. 70)
Eckhart, Meister, xxvi–xxvii, xxix,
lin42, lin44, lin47–48, 105n4, 112n1
(ch. 57), 113n4, 113n1 (ch. 61), 116n2
(ch. 78), 121n2, 121n4, 123n5
Elisabeth of Hungary, xxxiv
Elisabeth of Schönau, xiv
Elsbeth von Oye, xvi
Emmaus, 3
Engelport, xxxiii, xxxvi, liiin61
Epiphany, xvii, 41, 74, 85, 89, 109n1
(ch. 35), 109n2 (ch. 35), 116n1 (ch.
80), 120n1 (ch. 93), 121n1 (ch. 93),
121n1 (ch. 96)
Esther (Biblical figure), xxviii, 1;
book of the Bible, lvin87, 99n1
(ch. 1)

Ezekiel (book of the Bible), xxii,
lvin87, 105n7

Franciscan Order, xiii, xxvi, xxx,
107n2 (ch. 27)

Gertrude the Great of Helfta, ix,
xxi, xlviin24; *ein botte der götlichen
miltekeit*, 115n2 (ch. 72); *Legatus
divinae pietatis*, xxi, xlviin24, 115n2
(ch. 72), 118n3 (ch. 81)
Gisilher von Slatheim, xxvi, ln42
Gotsman, provost of Rothenkirchen,
xlviin19
Gregory the Great, xlviiin28, 11,
101n2 (ch. 9); saint's day, 118n1
(ch. 82)

Hadewijch, xx, 105n4, 105n5
Hane (convent), xv–xvi, xix, xxxiv–
xxxvii, xliv, liiin65, 1, 99n1 (head-
note), 101n1 (ch. 9), 103n1 (ch. 17),
106n4, 107n2 (ch. 27), 108n2 (32),
111n2 (ch. 51)
Heart, Divine, xix, xlviin22, 27, 43,
60, 86–87; of Jesus, xiv
Helfta, xix, xxi, xlvii
Hermann Joseph of Steinfeld, xiii–
xiv, xlvn4, 109n2 (ch. 32)
Hermann of Reichenau (Heriman-
nus Contractus), 107n1 (ch. 27)
Hertwig, Sister, 50, 52, 111n2 (ch. 51)
Hester, lin49
Holy Friday, 24
Hubyrechts, Frans, xxxvii, livn73,
Fig. 3
Hugh Ripelin of Strasbourg, xxvi,
122n2 (ch. 98)

Ilbenstadt, xxxiii, xxxvi
Imagina von Isenburg-Limburg,
106n1 (ch. 26)
Immaculate Conception, xxix–xxx

Jacob, Brother, 54
John (disciple of Jesus), 46
John, Gospel of, lvin87, 100n2 (ch. 5), 105n8, 108n3 (ch. 31), 110n1 (ch. 39), 110n2 (ch. 39), 119n2 (ch. 88), 122n3 (ch. 99)
John, the Baptist (biblical figure), 8; Before the Latin Gate, 48, 110n1 (ch. 45); Beheading of, 51, 69, 111n3, 116n1 (ch. 76); Nativity of, 29, 49, 68, 93, 106n1 (ch. 23), 111n1 (ch. 49), 116n1 (ch. 73), 122n1 (ch. 98)
John XXII, Pope, xlviiin27
Julian of Norwich, ix

Kempe, Margery, ix
Kings (books of the Bible), lvin87, 107n2 (ch. 29)
Königstein, xxxvi–xxxvii

Lahnstein, 32, 106n1 (ch. 26)
Langmann, Adelheid, xxi, ln39
Lauer, Caspar, xxxvi, lvn80
Lent, 21, 24
Luke, Gospel of, lvin87, 100n1 (ch. 3), 100n2 (ch. 3), 101n8, 103n2 (ch. 17), 109n1 (ch. 36), 110n2 (ch. 38), 122n2 (ch. 99), 122n3 (ch. 99), 123n6, 123n7

Mainz, city of, xli; Diocese of, xliv, 1, 99n1 (ch. 1)
Margarete of Engelsstadt, xxxv
Marquard of Lindau, xxx
Mary, Annunciation of, xx, 43, 65, 86, 95, 109n1 (ch. 37), 114n2 (ch. 67), 120n1 (ch. 95), 123n1; Assumption of, xxix, 34, 51, 69, 82, 107n1 (ch. 27), 197n1 (ch. 29), 111n1 (ch. 52), 116n1 (ch. 75), 119n1 (ch. 87); Nativity of, 35, 51, 82, 108n1 (ch. 30), 111n1 (ch. 53), 119n1 (ch. 88); Presentation of, 57, 112n1 (ch. 59);

Purificatio (Candlemas), 42, 47, 62, 85, 109n1 (ch. 36), 110n1 (ch. 41), 114n1 (ch. 64), 114n2 (ch. 64), 120n1 (ch. 94)
Mary Magdalene, 5; conversion legend of, xxxiii–xxxiv, liii, lvn75; Saint's day of, 50, 68, 81, 111n1 (ch. 51), 116n1 (ch. 74), 119n1 (ch. 86)
Mathew, Gospel of, lvin87, 101n2 (ch. 7), 102n2 (ch. 15), 110n2 (ch. 38), 112n4
Maundy Thursday, 48, 66, 110n1 (ch. 43), 115n1 (ch. 69)
Mechthild of Hackeborn, xxi; *Liber specialis gratiae*, xxi
Mechthild of Magdeburg, xx–xxi, 105n4; *Flowing Light of the Godhead*, xvi, xlvin12, 105n4
Mirabilis, Christina, xvi, xxiv, xlvin14, livn72
Mittermaier, Franz Paul, xv, xxxvi–xxxvii
Mortification, of the flesh, xiii, xvii–xviii, 13, 16–17, 51
Mount of Olives, 21
Music, ix, xiv, xxiii, xlixn32, xlixn33, 92, 105n8, 109n4; melody (tune), 29, 31, 38, 106n2 (ch. 24). *See also* Angels

Nassau, counts of, xv, 106n4
Nazareth, 2
Neidhart, xli, lvin84
Neoplatonism, xix, xxvi, xlviin21, 113n2, 123n4
Nicholas (saint's day), 58, 113n1 (ch. 60); Chapel of Saint, 21, 33–34, 42, 103n1 (ch. 17)
Nicolaus de Capua, xlixn32
Norbertines. *See* Premonstratensian Order
Norbert of Xanten, xv, xxxv, xxxix, xlvn7, livn73

Palatinate, xv, xx, xxxvi, lvii (map), 106n1 (ch. 26)

Palm tree, xxii, 35; *Palm Tree Treatise*, xlviiin29

Passion, of Christ, xviii, 21–24, 89, 92, 121n7

Passion Sunday, 66, 115n1 (ch. 68), 115n3

Paternoster, 5–6

Paul (apostle), xxviii, 13

Peasants' War, xxxv

Pentecost, xliv, 26–27, 49, 67, 80, 104n1 (ch. 21), 104n1 (ch. 22), 111n1 (ch. 47), 111n1 (ch. 48), 115n1 (ch. 72), 118n1 (ch. 85)

Pieter de Waghenare, xxxiv, xxxvi–xxxvii

Premonstratensian Order, xiii–xiv, xxxiii, xxxv, xxxvii, xxxix, xlii, 99n1 (headnote), 106n2 (ch. 25), 109n2 (ch. 32)

Proverbs (book of the Bible), lvin87, 111n4, 114n2 (ch. 65)

Psalms (book of the Bible), xliv, lvin87, 5, 100n1 (ch. 4), 100n4, 101n7

Purgatory, xviii, xxiv–xxv, xxviii, xxxvii–xxxviii, xlvin11, ln38, ln39, 13, 30, 35, 38–40, 53–55, 57, 60, 64, 67, 73, 79, 84, 87, 91

Radegund, 101n4

Reformation, xxxix

Retters, xxxvi–xxxvii, lvn74; Christina of, xxxvi, xxxxix

Revelation, of John, lvin87, 103n1 (ch. 16), 108n2 (ch. 31), 114n4, 115n2 (ch. 72)

Romans (book of the Bible), lvin87, 101n5

Rome (Vatican), xxii, 29, 106n2 (ch. 23)

Rommersdorf, xxxiii, xxxvii

Rothenkirchen, xv, xix, xlviin19

Rothschild Canticles, xxii, xlixn31

Ruh, Kurt, xiii, xx, xlvn1, xlviin23

Ruusbroec, Jan van, xxvi

Satan, 11–14

Sayn, xxxiii

Scotus, John Duns, xxix

Song of Songs, xxi, xxvii, lvin87, 22, 35, 103n3 (ch. 17), 108n2 (ch. 30)

Suso, Henry, ix, xxvii

speculum, 101n3 (ch. 9)

Speyer, diocese of, 99n1 (headnote)

Suso, Henry, ix, xxvii

Thessalonians (books of the Bible), lvin87, 103n1 (ch. 16)

Thomas of Cantimpré, xvi, xlvin14

Tobias (Saint), 12; Tobit (book of the Bible), lvin87, 101n1 (ch. 10)

Tree of Jesse, xxxix

Ulric of Augsburg (saint's day), 50, 111n1 (ch. 50)

Ursula (saint's day), 37, 52, 83, 108n1 (ch. 32), 109n2 (ch. 32), 112n1 (ch. 55), 119n1 (90)

William of Ware, xxix

Wisdom of Solomon (book of the Bible), lvin87, 101n2 (ch. 10)

Worringen, Battle of, xlin11, 30, 106n4

Valentine (saint's day), 63

Xerxes, 1

Zion, daughter of, 64